TEACHABLE MOMENTS

Using Everyday Encounters with Media and Culture
to Instill Conscience, Character, and Faith

Marybeth Hicks

HOWARD BOOKS
An Imprint of Simon & Schuster, Inc.
New York   Nashville   London   Toronto   Sydney   New Delhi

Howard Books
An Imprint of Simon & Schuster, Inc.
1230 Avenue of the Americas
New York, NY 10020

First Howard Books trade paperback edition August 2015

HOWARD and colophon are trademarks of Simon & Schuster, Inc.

For information about special discounts for bulk purchases,
please contact Simon & Schuster Special Sales at 1-866-506-1949
or business@simonandschuster.com.

The Simon & Schuster Speakers Bureau can bring authors to your live event.
For more information or to book an event, contact the Simon & Schuster Speakers
Bureau at 1-866-248-3049 or visit our website at www.simonspeakers.com.

Interior design by Davina Mock-Maniscalco

Manufactured in the United States of America

10   9   8   7   6   5   4   3   2   1

Library of Congress Cataloging-in-Publication Data

Hicks, Marybeth.
Teachable moments: using everyday encounters with media and culture to instill
conscience, character, and faith / Marybeth Hicks.
pages cm
Includes bibliographical references.
1. Parenting—Religious aspects—Christianity. 2. Child rearing—Religious aspects—
Christianity. 3. Mass media and children—United States. I. Title.
BV4529.H53 2014
248.8'45—dc23
2014003232

ISBN 978-1-4767-5743-8
ISBN 978-1-4767-5751-3 (pbk)
ISBN 978-1-4767-5750-6 (ebook)

For my mother,
whose prayers are always answered

Contents

TEACHABLE
MOMENTS

CHAPTER ONE

Parenting in the Moment

YOU ASK YOUR TEN-YEAR-OLD son to get the newspaper from the front porch. When he comes into the kitchen, he's reading a front-page story about a politician whose claim to fame is his predilection for "sexting" with young women, none of whom is his wife.

On the way to school, you pass a billboard that says EXTREME METH MAKEOVER, featuring before-and-after photos of a methamphetamine addict. Your kids want to know if this is a new reality TV show.

While your older children are at school, you take your four-year-old daughter with you to the grocery store. At the check out, she points to a magazine picture of a scantily clad Miley Cyrus "twerking" on stage and asks, "What is Miley doing?"

After school, you're the carpool driver. A fellow third grader tells your child all about last night's episode of *Glee*, which focused on a gay high school romance. You try to change the subject, so the kids tell you about a boy in their class who is being bullied. They're sure it's because he is gay.

At dinner, your eight-year-old hums Daft Punk's "Get Lucky" while your twelve-year-old mentions that the soccer coach dropped an f-bomb while yelling directions at the team.

It's just another day of parenthood in America, and another night in which you'll pray that God will help you to build a hedge of protection around your children before the culture steals their hearts away for good.

There's no way to avoid the intrusion of popular culture into our homes and families, but we don't have to let these instances exploit and influence our children. Instead, we can use those unplanned opportunities to instill conscience, character, and faith into the hearts and minds of the children God has entrusted to our care.

Educators use the phrase "teachable moments" to describe unforeseen and unexpected opportunities to veer away from a lesson plan in order to capitalize on something that sparks students' interest. Teachable moments sometimes arise from the day's headlines or from something that happens in pop culture. They can suggest themselves from something exciting that happens to an individual student, or from an unpleasant incident on the playground. The lessons these moments present aren't necessarily obvious, or even directly related to the incident itself. Essentially, teachable moments are springboards for learning—any kind of learning, about anything at all.

Intentional Parenting

Educators also use the term "intentional teacher." According to researcher and author Dr. Ann Epstein, intentional teachers "act purposefully, with a goal in mind and a plan for accomplishing it. Intentional teaching is not an accident. When an unexpected situation arises, as it always does, intentional teachers recognize a teaching opportunity and are able to take advantage of it."

Intentionality is crucial in parenting, too, especially if we hope to pass along the truth of the Gospel to our kids.

Years ago, my late mother-in-law, a lifelong educator, made an inadvertent comment that helped me to articulate the concept of intentionality. We were visiting her with our two eldest daughters, then four and two years old, and I disciplined them for some reason (who can remember why?). Grandma Nita came to the girls' defense and said, "You don't need to be so strict. Your girls are so good and so well-behaved!"

I smiled at her and said, "That's not actually dumb luck, you know!"

Lots of folks think having "good kids" is just that—luck. But intentional parenting means thinking ahead about the character traits and moral development that you want for your children.

If, by definition, teachable moments are unplanned and unexpected, intentional parents must be vigilant and prepared to recognize them and use them for good. In that sense, any occurrence throughout a typical day could represent a teachable moment. Some come from the outside world, and some develop naturally in your family's daily life.

External Moments

External moments are those presented by popular culture and current events. They come to us through the media.

American media—once a conduit to receive a limited menu of information and entertainment—is now a fixture in our daily lives, offering a diet of content that quickly overwhelms our limited capacity. Aside from causing nearly constant sensory overload, this ubiquitous media presence means that the people who control the messages that our children consume have pulled up a seat at the family table. Their ideas, opinions, worldviews, and values now are among those that shape and mold our children's character and conscience.

But media dissemination is no longer a one-way street; it's an interactive component woven into the fabric of our existence. It has changed not only our vocabulary, turning random nouns into verbs ("Facebook me!" "Text me!" "DM me!"), but also the ways we relate to our children and the ways they relate to the world. So as we look for teachable moments, we must not only address media consumption but also discuss the use of technology.

It will help to have some perspective about our kids' generation. Researchers sometimes refer to our children as "Generation M"—Generation Media. In its study about the media habits of children aged eight to eighteen, the Kaiser Family Foundation found in 2010 that young Americans spend an average of seven hours and thirty-eight minutes per day engaged with media. The study also calculated media multi-tasking (surfing the net while watching TV, for example), which increased the total average media time to ten hours and forty-five minutes per day. And this didn't even include texting!

Parents should be concerned about the amount of time our children spend with media. Study after study proves that the content of our modern media is influencing and molding our children's character and values. Behaviors related to sex, violence, substance use, consumerism, body image, and interpersonal relationships are modeled in the media with alarming impact. But just as importantly, our children's attitudes and opinions are formed based on the manner in which important subjects are portrayed in popular culture, and these ideas often are contrary to the tenets of Christianity. Given the conflicting moral messages with which they are constantly confronted, it's no wonder children and teens are confused or indifferent about how to live the Gospel values.

Still, it's important to remember that technology itself is morally neutral. Just as it can be used to compromise or even corrupt their souls, it also can be a tool to teach and promote the lessons our children need to live moral and faithful lives. Media devices can isolate us from one another, but if we use them in a positive way, they can bring us together. The trick is to have mastery over our media consumption, and not let media have mastery over us.

Organic Moments

It's not just the outside world as experienced through the media that offers teachable moments. Teachable moments also come simply from living our lives. Family relationships and friendships, sports and extracurricular activities, and episodes of growth and maturity create opportunities to teach valuable lessons. The American ethos itself has morphed in ways that require families to face delicate, difficult, and even dangerous realities. Venturing out into the community with our kids means confronting inadvertent exposure to behaviors and situations we'd rather they didn't hear or see.

Imagine:

Waiting for a table at the chicken wing joint on a Sunday evening after church, trying to ignore a group of college guys comparing notes about the drunken debauchery they experienced the night before.

Or walking past the toy aisles at Walmart as a mom yells at her son, "Get the (bleep) over here!"

Or sitting with your son in the waiting room of an urgent care clinic and being forced to overhear a stranger describe her personal medical issues to her boyfriend over her cell phone.

Not that any of these things ever happened to my family!

Each of these scenarios is a teachable moment. Intentional parents can use everything—cultural intrusions, gritty or awkward encounters, and personal triumphs and hardships—to communicate about what's important.

There's another reason why teachable moments are so critical: *not* infusing our values and beliefs into those moments sends an equally powerful message that the values of the dominant popular culture are A-okay with you.

To be sure, many teachable moments will feel excruciating to you and your kids. It's not always comfortable to address the incidents that come to our attention. But if we're going to fulfill our obligations as parents, ignoring them isn't an option. The alternative is a society where the moral void in the hearts of our children is filled with relativism, superficiality, and even wickedness. Here's a tragic example of what I mean.

A Cautionary Tale: Absent a Compass

In September 2010, Rutgers University freshman Tyler Clementi, aged eighteen, took his own life by jumping off the George Washington Bridge. Tyler had discovered that his roommate, Dharun Ravi, had spied on him during a gay sexual encounter by using a webcam in their shared dorm room. Worse, Dharun had invited others to watch along with him.

Dharun, an immature and morally inept young adult, was sentenced to only thirty days in prison, followed by three years of probation, three thousand hours of community service, and training about the use of technology and "alternative lifestyles." He could have gone to jail for ten years for creating the humiliation and emotional distress that appears to have been the reason for Tyler's suicide, but the judge apparently determined that his motives weren't evil, just infantile.

Dharun's conviction for invasion of privacy, bias intimidation, and tampering with a witness and evidence in the aftermath of Tyler's death revealed the complete bankruptcy of conscience with which he operated. (He attempted to delete certain texts and online communications in an apparent effort to mitigate his role in causing his roommate's emotional state).

Punctuating the case, juror Lynn Audet said after the verdict, "Deletion is futile. Text messages, tweets, emails, iChats are never gone. Be careful. I've already told my kids, be careful. If you're going to put something in writing, be able to back it up."

Underscoring the superficial morality that guides our nation's youngest generation, the best we can come up with seems to be: "Your love of technology may come back to bite you in the butt, so watch what you say in cyberspace."

Not exactly the lesson I would be going for in such a teachable moment.

When the story of Tyler Clementi's sad suicide made headlines, I discussed it with my then–middle school daughter. When I told her that one roommate had invaded another's privacy in such a brash and callous way, her indignant response was, "Who DOES that?"

One answer says it was Dharun, the immature college boy. He wasn't malicious, his defense attorney said, but rather he meant to "pwn" (a purposeful misspelling of the word "own"—to pwn someone is to more than just own them) his roommate with a thoughtless prank. A prank? Really?

The alternative explanation—the one that gained so much traction in the media after Tyler's death—is that Dharun exemplified the intolerance of homosexuality that prompts the bullying now epidemic across our country. Not to sound cynical, but that was a convenient conclusion for the folks promoting the gay agenda, despite the fact that Dharun had plenty of gay friends to vouch for his open-mindedness.

This was my brash conclusion: Dharun wasn't a homophobe or a prankster. He was a kid without a moral compass.

People with a well-developed conscience know that it is always wrong to invade the privacy of another person. Moreover, they are capable of holding whatever opinion they choose about another person without acting on that opinion, whether the issue is sexuality or race or obesity or intelligence or gender. You may dislike someone because that person looks at you funny or has an obnoxious laugh or is smarter than you. You just can't torment him or her. That's wrong. It's always wrong, no matter why you do it.

Put another way, there are some things you just don't do.

This is what's known as a moral imperative. Unfortunately, Dharun's moral compass—the thing that should have pointed him toward true north and a path of correct behavior—was as immature as his ultimate course of action.

This sort of senseless, heartless episode is what happens when human beings are not molded in conscience and character. Because, as my then-twelve-year-old succinctly put it, good people don't do things like that.

The Character Crisis

We're all about "crises" in our country. In the past several years, we've had a credit crisis, a housing crisis, and an employment crisis, and soon we're expecting a student loan crisis. These social and political calamities always get their own logos and theme songs on the news. That's how you know it's a "crisis."

Despite the seriousness of these social disasters, they don't compare to the real catastrophe we face: the crisis of our children's character, as evidenced by the behavior of Dharun Ravi in the death of Tyler Clementi. I picked their story because it is shocking and tragic, and it ought to be inconceivable. But I could have used the story of the thirteen- and fourteen-year-old boys in East Harlem who tossed a shopping cart off a four-story walkway—for fun—hitting an innocent wife and mother walking below, who happened to be buying Halloween candy for underprivileged children. She was in a medically induced coma for a while and permanently lost her vision in one eye, but in court the boys said they were sorry, so there's that.

Or I could have used the humiliating incident of the physically mature eleven-year-old Pennsylvania girl caught "sexting" topless photos of herself to her classmates. The parent of one of the recipients of her nude photos alerted authorities, who contacted the girl's parents, who of course had no clue their not-even-teenage-daughter was doing such a thing.

Or I could have told the heart-wrenching tale of the Connecticut Boy Scout who committed suicide on the first day of school after years of bullying by his classmates. A friend described the boy as quirky and odd. He was from Poland and had only lived in the US for a few brutal and humiliating years, so maybe the kids at school were still trying to get to know him.

These stories and others like them make me ask myself: Where are we going, and why are we in this handbasket?

To be sure, some studies, such as those conducted by the Pew Research Center's Religion and Public Life Project, claim that today's young adults are not morally insufficient, but in fact share the moral and religious opinions of their elders. Statistics such as "76 percent of eighteen- to twenty-nine-year-olds believe there are absolute standards of right and wrong" prompted at least one snarky editorial to note that those who are worried about moral decay in our country are just overreacting. And we're not hip, either.

Unfortunately, opinion research doesn't jibe with studies about the behavior and habits of young people. To put it bluntly, a large swath of America's young people wouldn't know right or wrong if it took a bite out of their corndog. Teens and young adults are so ingrained in the mind-set of relativism that they mostly believe the notions of right and wrong, and even the concept of "truth," are "personal," as in, you have "your truth" and I have "my truth."

Dr. Christian Smith, professor of sociology at the University of Notre Dame, conducted studies that show that many young people lack even a vocabulary for morality. Instead of framing their actions and beliefs in the context of "right" and "wrong," they couch their morality in emotion and relativism. If something feels bad, then it's probably wrong. If it feels good, it's right. Something can feel bad to you and be wrong for you, but if it feels good to someone else, it's right for that person. And evaluating behavior choices means assessing an action on the basis of how it might make someone else feel, not whether the behavior is innately right or wrong.

The problem with using feelings as the arbiter for assessing moral behavior is that not everyone feels the same way. Emotions make for a moving target; they change from person to person, and even from day to day. Empathy, or even a consistent application of the Golden Rule, can guide our actions, but it doesn't define morality. For example, we don't avoid lying because being deceived might hurt someone's feelings; we avoid it because lying is simply wrong, whether or not it hurts another person.

Longitudinal studies by the Josephson Institute of Ethics prove that a crisis in moral development exists among teens. In its biennial study of twenty-three thousand high school students, the organization has found that unethical behavior on the part of young people is "entrenched." Among other findings, in 2012 the Josephson Institute found:

- While 86 percent of boys and 95 percent of girls believe that being a good person is more important than being rich, 23 percent of boys and 17 percent of girls admitted stealing from a store within the past year. Moreover, nearly half of boys—45 percent—agreed with the statement "A person has to lie and cheat at least occasionally in order to succeed." Twenty-eight percent of girls also held this cynical belief.

- Nearly 20 percent of boys *disagreed* with the statement "It's not worth it to cheat because it hurts your character." But 20 percent of boys agreed with the statement "It's not cheating if everyone is doing it." Ten percent of girls shared those opinions.

- Rampant cheating in school continues. A majority of students (51 percent) admitted cheating on a test during the last year. One in three admitted they used the Internet to plagiarize an assignment.

Alarmingly, despite evidence that cheating, lying, and stealing are common behaviors, fully 93 percent of students surveyed said they were satisfied with their ethics and character, and 99 percent said having good character is very important. Eighty-one percent believe that when it comes to doing what is right, they are better than most people they know—proving that while some American kids may not have a moral compass, they do have excellent self-esteem!

How did we get to a point where our children seem to make no connection between their behavior and the character it reflects? If this doesn't define a crisis in character, what would?

For years, I've argued that this "disconnect" stems from the parenting trend to reinforce self-esteem at all costs, irrespective of how a kid behaves, rather than connect self-esteem to goodness. Kids should feel good about themselves when they *are* good, when they do the right things and make moral choices.

But parents are warned to correct their children's *behavior*, not their children, on the grounds that their kids might feel bad about themselves. Isn't that exactly what a conscience is meant to do—make us feel badly when we do the wrong thing? That's the purpose of guilt and shame, two old-fashioned and denigrated emotions that must make a comeback if we're going to rescue our children's generation.

All kids make mistakes and do dumb, hurtful things. The current parenting style in our nation is to respond like this: "Charlie, I know you didn't mean to steal your brother's Halloween candy, tear up his homework, and put his iPod in the dishwasher. Those were just poor choices that made your brother sad. Tomorrow, you can have a fresh start and make better choices that don't hurt his feelings. But you're still a great person and nothing you ever do will change that." Such parenting is evidence of the truism, "Even a felon is loved by his mother."

To connect our children's behavior to their character is to give meaning to their choices beyond just the unpleasant outcome of hurting someone else's feelings (which may or may not bother a child!). A more useful response for moral education is: "Wow, Charlie, I don't know if you intended to hurt your brother's feelings and destroy his property, or if you were just acting impulsively. Either way, your behavior tells me that your character needs work. People who deliberately hurt others are known as insensitive and cruel, or at the very least, rude. And people who deliberately ruin the property of others are known as selfish, thoughtless, or even destructive. People will decide if you're a good boy or a bad boy by the way you behave. If you're a good boy, your behavior will show everyone what kind of character you have."

Should you call Charlie a bad boy? Of course not! But you should certainly make sure he understands that his actions speak for his character. If that sounds like he's a bad boy . . . well . . . that's for Charlie's budding conscience to decide.

Many bright minds are writing about the genesis of this moral void in America's youth. Radio host and author Dennis Prager blames the decline in religious belief for waning moral intelligence in our culture generally, and certainly in our young people. The Pew Research study, despite its rosy picture of generational morality, quantifies the waning religiosity of young Americans.

Why is this important to note? Because without a religious foundation, our young people's morality is essentially a personal behavior code.

Where this all started is anybody's guess. It could be rooted in the materialistic, spoiled parenting experienced by Baby Boomers at the hands of their well-meaning but newly affluent moms and dads, or it might be linked to the sexual and cultural upheaval of the sixties and seventies. Perhaps it was caused by feminism and the resultant change in the roles of parents in the daily lives of their children, or it might be the upshot of aggressive sociopolitical progressivism that has marginalized religion in the public square.

Don't know . . . can't say. No matter the cause, our kids' generation suffers for want of a guiding moral compass.

It's not the statistics that ought to convince us, though, or even the troubling stories that dominate the media. What ought to persuade us that there is a disturbing moral vacuum are the examples we find in our daily experience.

Think I'm exaggerating? Read your child's Twitter feed. I read my daughter's and discovered that a popular boy in our community was promoting the moral corruption of hundreds of teens, making it look cool and fun to live a totally amoral life.

This is the environment in which we are called to instill Gospel values into the hearts and minds of our children. No wonder we're struggling!

Carpe Articulum! (Seize the Moment!)

What next? How can you put into practice the idea of "teachable moments" to assure you're doing enough to build your child's moral intelligence? A few concrete strategies will help you become accustomed to incorporating lessons about conscience, character, and faith into your daily interactions with your children:

Be intentional and look for teachable moments. Acting intentionally and staying alert for teachable moments gives us the opportunity to weave lessons about character, virtue, faith, and values into our everyday conversations with our kids.

For instance, when I was talking with my daughter, Amy, about the students at Rutgers University, it prompted an interesting and insightful conversation with her. When Amy asked indignantly "Who *DOES* that?" about Dharun Ravi's despicable "prank," I replied, "Why do you say that?" She then explained to me—in middle school terms—the moral imperatives about respecting others' privacy (even if you don't approve of what they're doing), protecting the feelings of others, avoiding behavior that you know is harmful to others, and accepting responsibility for your actions.

Rather than simply comment on how sad the story was, I used it to encourage my daughter to think about the missing elements of morality that allowed the tragedy to happen in the first place. Mind you, this conversation took place on the ten-minute drive from our house to school. This demonstrates how moral lessons ought to be taught to children—in the moment. The goal isn't to sit down for a formal presentation about moral behavior or belabor the point, but to routinely incorporate such discussions into your conversation.

Now think back to that typical parenting day at the beginning of this chapter—the one that starts with the news story about a "sexting" scandal and ends with a soccer coach using vulgarity at practice. How might you take those moments and turn them into something useful and good for your children? What can you do to capitalize on those instances when it seems your children's innocence is being hijacked and their character influenced by the wrong things?

When your son hands you the paper and you read the headline about a public scandal, frame the story in moral terms. "It's so disappointing to see public figures acting without integrity," you might say. "Politicians lose their moral leadership by behaving this way.

And 'sexting' always exploits someone, which makes it a truly hurtful act." Moral lesson accomplished. Pour the coffee.

Learning that a coach used vulgarity when speaking to the soccer team might generate a similar discussion: "Coaches and teachers have a responsibility to model respectful behavior for their players and students. Do you think your coach's language set a good example? Was it respectful to the team? What impression does he leave with you when he uses words like that?" In instances like this, you can demonstrate how others judge someone's character based on their actions.

Define what's right and what's wrong. First things first. Teaching morality to our children begins with the simple truth that God created the universe and everything in it; that every person is created in the image and likeness of God, possessing dignity and worth; and that God loves everything he creates. For Christians, this is the basis for a moral code that has been revealed to us directly, through biblical instruction, as well as personally, by understanding the character of God in the person of Jesus Christ.

To summarize: to be a moral person is to be Christlike. Which also explains why it's so darn hard.

Our Christian moral code tells us what is right and wrong in the context of our faith, which we know to be based on truth. Jesus gave us an excellent reminder of just what our foundation must be. Everyone assumes it's the "Golden Rule" —"Do unto others as you would have them do unto you"—but the foundation for our moral lives is Jesus's Great Commandment:

"Love the Lord your God with all your heart and with all your soul and with all your mind." This is the first and greatest commandment. And the second is like it: "Love your neighbor as yourself." All the Law and the Prophets hang on these two commandments.

(Matthew 22:37–40)

Morality, then, is a system of behavior that reflects our love of God and demonstrates that love in the Christlike treatment of others.

Very young children need concrete terms in order to categorize their actions. Parents often tell children a behavior is "inappropriate," but don't grasp what this means. It implies knowledge of a community standard about appropriateness, which even many adults don't have. When teaching little ones about moral behavior, it's best to use the simple words "right," "wrong," "good," and "bad."

Kids also respond well when we use direct language to describe specific immoral behaviors. If someone cheats on a test at school, that person is a "cheater." Someone who lies is a "liar." Someone who steals is a "thief." Children can understand that certain bad actions identify your character in unflattering—but accurate—ways.

Older children and teens need a more precise vocabulary to help them assess the behavior they observe as well as the actions they contemplate for themselves.

When philosophers want to talk about something that's wrong, they use the word "impermissible," meaning the behavior is something that isn't allowed; you aren't supposed to do it. When they want to talk about something that's right, they might use the word "permissible," which means it *is* allowed and you *may* do it. But they also might use the word "obligatory," which describes something you really ought to do (or perhaps it is something you ought never to do). Developing a conscience revolves around understanding the "oughtness" of things—knowing what things we must do, and what we mustn't.

Define good character. We also need to teach words that describe the character traits we hope to cultivate in our children. Parents of wee ones tend to speak in terms of being "good" or being "nice," but these words are nebulous. There are better, more specific terms, like being "obedient"—doing what you're told—and being "kind"—acting thoughtfully and considerately toward others. These precise words can easily be taught to toddlers and preschoolers.

The older they get, the more specifically children need to know the traits that will mark them as persons of good character. This may sound simplistic, but we can't assume that children know what constitutes virtue. In fact, in our culture, "good" and "nice" are about as far as we go in describing a person's positive traits.

This isn't an exhaustive list by any means, but the words below precisely define the character we want to instill in our children and the traits we want them to exhibit in their attitudes, intentions, and actions:

Accountable	Committed	Dependable
Appreciative	Compassionate	Discerning
Benevolent	Confident	Disciplined
Brave	Considerate	Empathetic
Caring	Content	Enthusiastic
Charitable	Cooperative	Faithful
Chaste	Courteous	Focused

Forgiving	Kind	Reverent
Friendly	Loving	Righteous
Frugal	Loyal	Selfless
Generous	Magnanimous	Sensitive
Gentle	Merciful	Sincere
Gracious	Moderate	Steadfast
Grateful	Modest	Strong
Helpful	Obedient	Tactful
Honest	Patient	Temperate
Honorable	Peaceful	Tolerant
Hopeful	Persistent	Tough
Humble	Pious	Trusting
Idealistic	Prudent	Trustworthy
Industrious	Reliable	Truthful
Innocent	Resourceful	Wise
Joyful	Respectful	
Just	Restrained	

Make these words part of your vocabulary when you are talking with older children about their own or others' attitudes and actions.

Focus on the future. The work of parenting is to mold our children's character for adulthood, not simply to manage their experiences for success or happiness in the present day. It's tempting to try to fix things for our kids to make life easier for them, but often the best thing we can do is allow our children to experience the adversity brought on by their actions or the actions of others. There's an adage that reminds us of where our focus should be. My sister-in-law, Catherine, gave me a lovely tile with these words on it that I kept in my kitchen until my busy son, Jimmy, accidentally broke it: "Prepare the child for the path, not the path for the child." Whenever it's tempting to smooth things over, help your child avoid the natural consequences of his actions, or "level the playing field" in ways that require your adult intervention, consider what's really best for your child—your quick fix, or the capacity to handle whatever comes his or her way in life? When you keep the focus on the future, you'll more readily know how to respond in any given situation.

Teach by example. We parents also face moral choices each and every day, and we teach best when we demonstrate moral behavior by example. Any time our circumstances allow us to share our decision-making process with our kids, we can make a profound impact on them by showing them what it looks like when adults behave morally. It's one thing to tell your children to be scrupulously honest. It's another to take them with you back to the store to pay for something you inadvertently left on the lower rack of your shopping cart and didn't scan. Our actions speak volumes about our own moral fiber and convey to our children that virtue is a lifelong pursuit.

Every Family Is Different—Except When We're Alike

Families are unique, dynamic, and organic groups handpicked by God to join members together in a life-giving and eternal relationship. Other than that, we're pretty much all the same. We struggle with the same typical behaviors; we share the same doubts and make the same basic discoveries as we journey through the ages and stages of family life. These days, we're also faced with the same questions and concerns about a culture that is making it more difficult to parent our children according to our core beliefs.

Situations that arise from family life, friendships, media use, school, sports, and "real world" experiences all offer opportunities to impart your parental wisdom, teach your values, instill your faith, and mold your children's character and conscience. In the pages that follow, you'll find common questions that moms and dads confront in their everyday encounters with the culture, along with my reflections and suggestions about how you might respond. There aren't any right answers—this isn't a "how to" book with specific directions; rather, it's a guide to help you think more strategically about ways to achieve your important parenting objectives.

Parenting books resonate with moms and dads precisely because our experiences are so universal. The goal of this book is offer the benefit of my years in the parenting trenches, as well as the insights I've gleaned as a culture commentator. To be clear, I'm not a parenting "expert" by training or degree, but I'm the indisputable authority on the four incredible people the good Lord put in my maternal care, and they have presented me with more teachable moments than I can ever recollect. If the thoughts and ideas that follow are helpful to you, I think we all know who gets the credit.

CHAPTER TWO

Teachable Family Moments

NOWHERE WILL OUR CHILDREN learn more about building excellent character and living lives of virtue than within the walls of the places we call home. As our children's first and most influential teachers, we parents hold a unique—and awesome!—responsibility to give them all the tools they need to face whatever comes their way in life.

Our culture would have us believe that those tools are something we can buy. If we don't succumb to that notion, we may nonetheless become caught up in the idea that giving our children opportunities to become high achievers is the path to future success and security. And certainly, since we want our kids to enjoy happy childhoods and to do well, we're willing to provide all the material comforts and extracurricular experiences we can.

But such things aren't the tools that will serve them in good stead. Proverbs 22:6 reminds us, "Train up a child in the way he should go; even when he is old he will not depart from it." God asks us to mold and form our children to live moral lives that fulfill his purposes for them. Oddly enough, no one needs a smartphone in the sixth grade in order to become a person of strong moral character!

Ages and Stages of Moral Development

Our instruction about character and moral development must be age-appropriate. This is not just so our kids will understand what we're talking about, but also because moral intelligence should be built on a solid foundation of basic ideas that are expanded upon as children grow in maturity and understanding.

Children ages two to seven can understand concepts of right and wrong, good and bad, and can also be taught to employ empathy in the way they treat others. They can understand what it means to have respect for others, especially respecting one's elders, as well as having respect for themselves and for those who are different from them. Little ones can learn to be kind. This is the time to form habits around teaching moral lessons through everyday experiences.

Children ages seven to twelve can understand concepts of responsibility, accountability, modesty, self-discipline, perseverance, and humility. During these crucial formative years, your children should be able to reiterate your values on a wide range of issues. They should know what you expect of them in most situations, even if they don't always do what you would like.

Adolescents aged thirteen to eighteen can act as moral agents in any situation they might encounter. Aside from knowing the "oughtness" of their behavioral choices, they can understand concepts of ambiguity, situational ethics, moral relativism, and moral reasoning. Given a potentially compromising scenario, they can apply not only the moral teaching you have provided but also the insight they have gleaned from church teaching, cultural examples, and societal norms.

Obedience versus Cooperation

For at least a generation, our culture has engaged in a style of parenting that's best described as "permissive." That's to say, parents permit lots of behaviors and don't exert much authority in the home. Even when these parents do attempt to give a directive, their children often aren't compliant. They know that if they don't obey, their parents aren't likely to do anything by way of discipline; there won't be an unpleasant consequence.

There was a time when obedience was the standard that parents expected when it came to their children's behavior. If Mom or Dad made a request, children did as they were told. It would be unthinkable that preschoolers, much less preteens, would say "No!" when their parents told them to do something. Then along came parenting experts urging us to seek our children's cooperation rather than demand their obedience. "Obedience" became a harsh word that implied mechanical children and militaristic parents, and a standard that was achieved by spanking and yelling. The new experts theorized that parents need not bend their children's will, but rather nurture their hearts and honor their spirits, thus leading to their willing cooperation.

I believe that expecting obedience in small things means we can teach cooperation in big things. If parents don't require obedience, but instead ask children to cooperate, we put the power into their hands to decide whether they will respect our authority. But when we demand obedience, we keep parental authority where it belongs—in the hands of parents, who know what is best for their children. As children grow older, we can approach our requests with mutuality, giving them the opportunity to act cooperatively with us, for example, in making social plans or deciding curfews. But even as our kids get older, we should expect them to respect our authority with obedience.

Homes in which obedience is the standard for children's behavior are more peaceful, more pleasant, and less emotive than homes in which parents are constantly negotiating, bribing, pleading, and threatening to get their children to cooperate. Obedience is a vital lesson that underlies other moral instruction. When children learn to obey their parents, they also learn that authority figures must be obeyed, from teachers and coaches to police officers and employers—not to mention, God!

Choosing Our Battles

Parents often tell me that they don't want to be in a constant state of conflict with their children, so rather than take a stand on every issue that comes along, they "choose their battles." This is sometimes a good strategy; I do it myself to a certain degree.

However, in our culture, it's clear that parents aren't choosing enough battles. For some, the desire to make peace with their kids means parents are not taking a stand on things that are truly important. Issues that seem insignificant, such as attire, using slang, watching popular TV shows, or listening to particular kinds of music, aren't necessarily going to make or break a child's character, but they will have an impact. During their formative years, your children need your guidance to make choices that reflect the values you're working to instill, and often these will be contrary to the trends or fads that seem attractive to a child or teen.

Over time, parents may discover they've chosen so few battles that they've lost the war against the culture's influence over their children's hearts and souls. This is why it's important to always assess whether you're choosing not to litigate an issue that is genuinely inconsequential, or just taking the path of least resistance to avoid conflict with your kids. It's vital to choose the battles that teach moral lessons and impact character development.

Instilling Virtue Versus Managing Behavior

Part of the notion of "choosing our battles" is the desire to manage children's behavior rather than use that behavior to teach valuable life lessons.

For example, all children tend to fight with their siblings. Parents would like to reduce this behavior, as it's annoying, unpleasant, and hurtful. In a management approach, parents would ask children to share a toy, give up the front seat in the van, give up a treat, or otherwise pacify their brother or sister in order to eliminate the unpleasantness. But parents who want to instill virtue might see a teachable moment and focus on the "oughtness" of treating that sibling lovingly, waiting for a turn, or sharing a treat or toy—even using the word "ought" to indicate that it's a moral obligation. Seeking to teach a moral lesson, parents can impart lessons about right and wrong in the way children treat their siblings, rather than just reduce the conflict that so commonly characterizes these relationships.

Much of the advice available to parents today focuses on behavior management techniques, and these techniques may produce a positive result, to be sure. But they don't necessarily teach fundamental lessons about how to *be*, rather than just how to behave. If behavior is an expression of underlying character, it's far more important to focus on the kind of person you're raising than on managing the outward behavior your child exhibits. Parenting in a manner that puts character development first means making decisions that are often very different from other parents' decisions.

Parenting by Proxy

In our culture, parents often go along with whatever it seems "everyone else" is doing, essentially parenting by proxy. It's a form of benign consent that causes families to drift into a lifestyle mandated by the whims and desires of popular child-leaders and the culture in which they are immersed.

When our children are young, it may be that most of the families around us are working to teach the same lessons we are about character, conscience, and faith. But then, before we know it, and without evaluating these decisions, we find ourselves following suit when families take paths we thought we would avoid. This style of parenting is the opposite of intentional; it's a way of relying on the culture and the community around us to instill their values instead of those that we profess to believe in.

Intentional parenting requires that we consider all of our decisions and determine what's best for our children and families, irrespective of what "everyone else" is doing. You may decide to do things around your house differently from the "norm," and that might be difficult, at least for a while. But children adjust quickly to the idea that their rules and family policies reflect the values and convictions of their parents, and within the limits that are imposed, they feel safe, secure, and well-loved.

Teachable moments at home arise each day in myriad ways. If some of these examples feel familiar, you're not alone . . .

Ten Teachable Family Moments

> You don't choose your family.
> They are God's gift to you, as you are to them.
> —ARCHBISHOP DESMOND TUTU

1. The moment: Your nine-year-old wants to know why Granny and Grandpa got divorced. Come to think of it, he'd like to know why he has four sets of grandparents and his friends have only two. And since everyone in the family seems to get divorced, are you planning on getting divorced too? And another thing: What's "rehab," and why did Uncle Steve have to go there? And what's a restraining order, anyway?

When kids starting asking about our families, things can get sticky! There are days we'd sooner answer the awkward question "How did that baby get inside there?" than the myriad questions children pose about the people we love.

How much you tell your children depends in large measure on their ages. There's no need to spoil a young child's innocence by explaining details of family dysfunction, just as there's no reason to hide from a teen the facts that comprise your family dynamic.

If you're concerned about protecting the privacy or reputation of your family members, be aware of how much you're talking in front of your children about the issues in your extended family. When children are toddlers and younger, parents get accustomed to speaking freely about anything and everything, only to discover that your now-four-year-old wants to know if Granny is still "on the wagon." Oops! Be sure that you always appreciate the incredible acuity of tiny ears.

An unspoken but important undercurrent is that children want reassurance. They want to know that just because their grandparents or other relatives have divorced doesn't mean you will. Your teachable moments should include reassurance that you are committed to a lifelong marriage, through good times and bad.

Until your children are about eight years old, your explanations should be broad and supportive, focused on the love that holds families together, especially in tough times. You might say, "Your grandparents had some hard times, and they just couldn't figure out how to get along in their home, so they decided to live apart. But they both love me, and they're both still an important part of my life. I learned a lot from them about how to have a strong family, and that's what I'm committed to doing."

When children reach adolescence and beyond, and perhaps glean some of the family history, it's best to answer their questions with straightforward information and strong moral teaching. You don't need to go into raw detail about all the behaviors or situations you witnessed (if they were upsetting to you as a child, they will be upsetting to your own children, as well). But you can certainly talk about how God's love has helped you to understand that destructive behaviors hurt families, and that Jesus's example of love and forgiveness is the model for your own family.

Complex, blended families are the stuff of real life in modern America, but that doesn't mean we ought not teach our children about the ideals for family life that God intends for us. You can talk about your families of origin honestly and openly, all the while weaving through your explanations the values of forgiveness, forbearance, and faithfulness that are the foundation of your family today.

> **In a big family the first child
> is kind of like the first pancake.
> If it's not perfect, that's okay;
> there are a lot more coming along.**
> —JUSTICE ANTONIN SCALIA

2. The moment: Your seven-year-old comes strutting from the bathroom with a full face of make-up. She's tied her top up with a hair tie so it reveals her tummy, and her shorts are rolled down, cheerleader style. When you ask why she's dressed this way, she says she wants to look cool,

like her older sisters. You're stymied. Your older daughters were wholesome and innocent when they were her age. Now that they're young teens, they are appropriately modest, but the house skews "older" since there are plenty of pop songs, fashion magazines, and conversations about high school interests. How can you get the genie back in the bottle with your youngest, who seems like she's "seven going on seventeen"?

A wise mom of four daughters once joked to me that her youngest was the girl she never would have let play with her eldest—and my husband and I understood exactly what she meant! In fact, our older daughters insist my husband and I have gotten "soft" as we've grown older. I prefer to use the world *adaptable*. I've also reminded my older children that a family is a dynamic organization. It changes dramatically as it grows and matures, and you can't make time stand still for the children at the end of the roster.

When our older girls were little, the house revolved around their age-appropriate interests and entertainment. They didn't grow up in a home full of teenagers, whose pop music offered the soundtrack for high school dances, cross-country team dinners, and "teen angst." Yet that's the environment their little sister experienced.

Like it or not, younger children generally can't avoid exposure to at least some of the teen lifestyle, and because they emulate their older siblings, they naturally pick up on it. Thus, your seven-year-old is molding herself into a savvy little sis who can run with the big girls, make-up and all.

Some parents are tempted to think this kind of "dress up" is cute and inconsequential, but the reality is that our culture is stealing the innocence of little girls. If you question whether the hyper-sexualizing of American childhood is a real problem, ask yourself why clothes designers make padded bras and skimpy underwear for girls aged seven to fourteen, and why the media seems to celebrate the risqué or compromising behavior of the celebrities that our children admire most. It's all part of bombarding kids with messages about sex and sexuality.

For your seven-year-old, teachable moments present themselves every time you send her to the bathroom to wash that make-up off her face. You can explain, "If you admire your older sisters, try to *be* like them! I really appreciate that they are modest and respectful in the way they dress and act."

Of course, younger siblings aren't just watching their older sisters and brothers—they're watching *with* them, too. TV, that is. With older kids comes a plethora of media in the home to which younger siblings should not be exposed. The job of supervising the media in your home is challenging if you have kids of varying ages, but not impossible. It requires a family commitment to safeguard young children from content that corrupts them.

As for your older daughters, you can capitalize on this teachable moment by reminding them that when they were little, you protected them from exposure to things that were not appropriate for them. Now it's their turn to play a role in molding the character and conscience of their younger sister by doing things such as taking time to play games or pretend with her, watching "kid" movies together, baking cookies, riding bikes—generally, helping their little sis enjoy life as a seven-year-old!

There are pros and cons to every position in the family. Just ask my second daughter, Betsy, who was not permitted to attend a fourth-grade birthday party because the entertainment was the movie *Spider-Man*, rated PG-13. A few years later, on a rainy summer afternoon, I took my whole crew to see *Spider-Man 2*, including four-year-old Amy, who sat on my lap.

Okay, so maybe they have a point about my getting soft. In my defense: rain.

> **I choose gentleness. . . .**
> **Nothing is won by force. I choose to be gentle.**
> **If I raise my voice, may it be only in praise.**
> **If I clench my fist, may it be only in prayer.**
> **If I make a demand, may it be only of myself.**
>
> —MAX LUCADO

3. The moment: Your middle school son argues about going to church on Sundays. He used to enjoy Sunday school when he was little, but over the past few years has grown surly at the mere discussion of joining a youth group or attending services. You're panicked at the thought that he is rejecting Jesus. Should you force him to go with you (and endure his horrible attitude), or let him stay home?

As Christian parents, we all want our children to live as believers and experience the peace and joy of an intimate relationship with Jesus Christ. There's nothing more important than assuring—to the degree we're able—that the foundations of faith have been instilled in our children's hearts. So it's understandably troubling when children seem to reject the faith in which they are brought up.

Adolescence is a time of significant transition, and many young teens begin to question the things their parents have taught them. But rather than jump to the conclusion that your son is rejecting Christianity, learn what's really going on. It may be that in his mind, religion is about rules and restrictions, about being told what you *can't* do.

In this crucial teachable moment, remember that Jesus never forces himself on us; rather, he invites us to follow him. As parents of a young teen, you should also adopt a posture of "invitation" in the manner in which you present your faith. You also might look at your son's faith life across the years and ask him if he's ready to test the principles he has learned by doing things that also give him some independence. Mission trips and volunteer work in the community are great ways for a teen to expand his horizons while learning how Jesus works through us.

On the other hand, your son is a minor, and it's your home. Therefore, you can have rules about living there. If one of those rules is to attend church together as a family—cheerfully—that's a reasonable expectation that you should require. You can't force your child to absorb the message, but you can say, "I get that you don't want to go to church. But we're your parents, and we are requiring you to go. You don't have to believe everything you hear, but you must listen respectfully. You don't have to like it, but you must be courteous. When you move out of our home, you can make your own decision about church, but for now it is part of our family life and an expectation that we have for you." In this way, you can use even a surly teenage attitude as a teachable moment about demonstrating respectful, courteous behavior in any situation.

Still, the goal would be to gently explore the reasons why your son has developed a negative attitude about church, and to work toward resolving his misgivings with instruction, patience, and love. Imagine that Jesus were requiring *us* to go to church . . . he'd certainly be kind about it, wouldn't he?

> **A child who is allowed**
> **to be disrespectful to his parents**
> **will not have true respect for anyone.**
> —REV. BILLY GRAHAM

4. The moment: Your twelve-year-old daughter starts talking back. You know this is typical for her age, and when she does it at home you just ignore it. But now she is talking back to you when you're out together shopping or visiting friends and family. It's embarrassing, but you're afraid if you call her out on it, she will be even ruder and you'll both look bad. How can you deal with public disrespect from your tween?

To stop your daughter's rude behavior in public, you have to demand that she's respectful to you in private, too. Don't have differing standards for how she treats you and how she treats others. Teaching her to treat you respectfully (which, by the way, is so important that God made it number four on his list of ten "preferred" behaviors!) is a crucial way you will prepare her for adulthood.

Unfortunately, as a culture we've accepted the relatively new American assumption that all tweens and teens talk back, and that this is normal and appropriate. This notion is reinforced in the media, where sitcoms for kids depict tweens as all-knowing and worldly wise, while the adult characters are often buffoons who rely on the wisdom of children to navigate the world.

When my eldest daughter was nearing thirteen, I heard lots of warnings from well-meaning friends about the "teenage monster" that soon would be living in my home. Some said, *"You'll never know how dumb you are until you have a teenager."* Others cautioned me to put on my emotional armor, because tweens and teens say cruel and insensitive things to their parents. One seasoned mom told me not to worry, because "She'll be twenty-five before you know it!"

Even parenting experts promote this idea, advising moms and dads to expect back talk as a normal and necessary part of growing up. Here's what James Bozigar, LSW, coordinator of community relations and a licensed social worker at the Family Intervention Center at Pittsburgh's Children's Hospital, once said about teens talking back:

> Independence is another reason for children talking back. As children grow and become more independent, they have a need to assert more control over their own lives. Talking back can be a way for children to separate themselves from their parents. . . . Kids need to talk back, but they need ways to do it that aren't disruptive to your relationship.

Kids *need* to talk back? *Really?* And we need to *help them do it* in ways that aren't disruptive to our relationships? Somehow, generations of people managed to reach adulthood without snarking at their mothers and fathers, but in modern-day America, rudeness has become something we expect from adolescents. Rather than a second round of the "terrible twos," the process of "individuation" (a fancy word for "growing up") ought to reveal greater maturity, the ability to focus attention outwardly, and the capacity to control emotions and cope with challenges.

Ironically, the philosophy about adolescence that accepts behaviors such as rudeness, back talk, self-centeredness, and condescension as normal and age-appropriate actually *promotes* immaturity and emotionalism. In other words, if we buy into this expectation about tweens and teens, we're likely to get exactly what we pay for.

A truism about children's behavior is that they tend to meet our expectations. If, as they enter adolescence, we expect them to become cranky, rude, disrespectful, and disinterested in their relationships with us, they're likely to live up to that (low) standard of behavior. Worse, we're unlikely to demand anything better from them.

On the other hand, if we hold that bar up just a bit and let our kids know that we have higher expectations for their behavior—even during their hormonally charged adolescent years—we send the message, "I understand you're growing and trying to figure things out, but I have confidence that you can behave in a way that I find acceptable and you can be proud of."

Of course, adolescents want control over their decisions, and if we're doing our jobs as parents, we're setting limits. There's a natural tension there that can lead to sparks. But if we approach our children's adolescent years with a positive attitude and some clear guidelines, this can be one of the most enjoyable seasons of parenting.

Despite those admonitions from more experienced parents and

parenting experts, I always optimistically believed that my children and I could chart a different course, because I stayed focused on molding the sort of character that would promote respectful and courteous behavior. And sure enough, we busted the myth that all children are destined to become "Attila the Teen."

Here's how you can do the same:

- *Discuss the traits that reflect well on a person's character.* Frequently remind your tween that her behavior demonstrates the content of her character. Focus on being restrained, temperate, self-disciplined, and cooperative. Don't allow excuses such as being tired or hormonal for unacceptable outbursts; instead, expect and demand respectful communication even when a teen is feeling punky.

- *Decide that the "rude is normal" standard is unacceptable.* Communicate this to your tween. How? Simply tell your child, "Rude is not normal. It's just rude." Declare that you and your child aren't going to settle for less than the best you can be, and make a pact to treat each other with mutual respect.

- *Let your daughter know that she is free to communicate respectfully and advocate her point of view.* What she isn't free to do is slam doors, yell, talk back, cuss, or scream "I hate you." Those behaviors indicate immaturity, and won't convince you that your tween is ready for more freedom, privileges, input in decisions, and so on.

Mature, polite communication instills parental confidence.

- *Give her the chance to regroup.* At our house, a Steve Martin–esque "Excuuuuuse me?" sends the message that we'd like a change in attitude, reflected in a more respectful tone of voice. If your tween isn't capable of regrouping, let her know you'll be available to talk further when she's able to be more respectful. (Never engage with an over-emotional tween!)

- *Reward maturity and respect.* Thank your tween for being different from the "norm" and demonstrating good character through courteous and respectful speech.

Love is not an affectionate feeling, but a steady wish for the loved person's good as far as it may be obtained.

—C. S. LEWIS

5. The moment: You blow your top. Stress, hormones, and lack of sleep conspire to rob you of a positive attitude and loving disposition. Despite all of your admonitions to your children not to use a rough day as an excuse to be unpleasant or hurtful to others, you're now the poster mom for everything you don't want your children to do. In short, you've been a meanie. What should you do when you've had a "bad mom" day?

Pray for God's forgiveness, and then forgive yourself! Then, turn this into a humble and tender teachable moment by telling your children that you regret your behavior and asking them to forgive you, too. It's as simple as that.

The pressure to be perfect parents comes from some crazy cultural expectation that "good" moms and dads never shout or speak impatiently or lose their tempers. Whether this started with an unrealistic TV version of "perfect parents" ("*Harriet! I'm home!*"), or is the result of reading too many parenting magazines at the pediatrician's office, we all must recognize that perfection in parenting (or life) is just not possible.

It's probable that the things you pitched a fit over are legitimate issues that you need to address. If you ask your kids to pick up their rooms, put away toys, or empty the dishwasher and they don't obey your directions, it's fair to be upset about their noncompliance. So be sure you distinguish between the subject of your tirade and the manner in which you expressed your displeasure.

I don't know any perfect parents. I haven't been one, that's for sure! When the fuse burns too quickly, we can turn those episodes into teachable moments about being accountable for our actions and seeking forgiveness. Find a quiet time to say, "I'm sorry for being so impatient today. I know my tone of voice was harsh, and I should have spoken more kindly. I'm still annoyed about (insert kid behavior here), but I hope you'll forgive the way I spoke to you today. Even adults can fall short of the standards of behavior we set for ourselves, but I can do better." Of course, always follow an apology with a hug.

A funny thing about children: they can't wait to forgive our mistakes and feel better about their relationships with their parents.

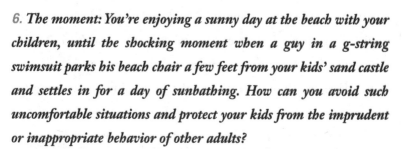

When you don't know what you're doing,
it's best to do it quickly.
—JASE ROBERTSON

6. The moment: You're enjoying a sunny day at the beach with your children, until the shocking moment when a guy in a g-string swimsuit parks his beach chair a few feet from your kids' sand castle and settles in for a day of sunbathing. How can you avoid such uncomfortable situations and protect your kids from the imprudent or inappropriate behavior of other adults?

Try as we might to enjoy wholesome family fun, it seems there's always a nude sunbather, a young couple engaging in too much "PDA," or a cussing grandpa to hijack the atmosphere and force us into scenes fit for an R-rated movie.

I remember a day at the beach when my children were young. My son and his buddy took a walk along the shore, only to discover a colony of nude sunbathers. They reported their findings: aging hippies were naked on the sand! Uncontrollable giggling ensued. Suffice it to say, for the rest of the day we took our beach strolls in the opposite direction.

Thanks to the culture in which we live, perfect strangers present us with possible teachable moments just about every day: People dropping "f-bombs" at ball games or in line at the superstore, vulgar T-shirts that draw stares from your kids, bumper stickers and decals that turn cars into mobile assault vehicles that attack your sensibilities, teens swapping spit at the movies. You can't avoid the constant barrage of behaviors that you'd like your kids not to emulate.

Resolving the situation isn't always possible, but creative moms and dads can find ways to regain the wholesome atmosphere you set out to enjoy. Avoid confrontation if you can, though sometimes a situation calls for a courteous request: "Would you mind watching your language, since you're sitting so close to children?" If your goal is to preserve the environment for your kids, your best bet is to move to a different location.

The situation becomes a teachable moment later. In the car on the ride home or while getting ready for bed, you can put whatever behavior you observed into the proper context. For example, you might mention that the fellow on the beach was wearing an immodest bathing suit that made you feel uncomfortable, and you thought it best to move. What would follow is a conversation about modesty and the importance of demonstrating respect for others and ourselves by dressing in ways that honor God's gift of dignity.

You might ask your kids, "What do you suppose that guy's image is intended to project? Do you think people assume good or bad things about him? Do you think his image helps him or hurts him? Do you think it's fair of us to pass judgment on someone who dresses immodestly?"

Lessons about character and conscience can be found in every awkward circumstance. The trick is to make the observation useful, rather than judgmental. It's easy to pass judgment on a grungy teenage guy with gauged ears, facial piercings, multiple tattoos, and a T-shirt with graphic words or images on it. But doing so would be wrong. And also, a young man just like that waited on me at the shoe store, and he was truly lovely.

Here's what I don't do when confronted with unpleasant or rude behavior: I don't just ignore it or pretend I didn't notice. Our culture has desensitized us to behaviors that ought to bother us. As parents, our response to the situations that offend us can become great teaching tools about how to be considerate of others and how to behave in ways that reflect our values.

> **Too many people spend money**
> **they haven't earned**
> **to buy things they don't want**
> **to impress people they don't like.**
> —WILL ROGERS

7. The moment: You feel like you just can't keep up with family or friends when it comes to buying all the latest gadgetry, shoes, clothes, and games for your kids. While it seems everyone you know takes an expensive vacation for spring break, as well as a long trip to the beach each summer, you can only afford a camping trip, and not on every school break. You don't feel poor by any means—you are blessed with good jobs and a nice home— but you can't afford to give your children the luxury items that their cousins and friends have. More importantly, you don't know if you would buy some of these things even if you could afford them. How can you frame conversations about money so that your kids understand your values?

When it comes to teaching about our Christian values, the earning, saving, and spending of money can be turned into some of the most fruitful teachable moments. There's hardly an issue or situation that arises that doesn't have some financial component, so the topic of money may come up anytime, in any circumstance.

The Bible is chock-full of references to money in both the Old and New Testaments, because money can so quickly lead us down paths that take us away from a life in Christ. Adopting an appropriate attitude about money and using it properly can lead to blessings of abundance and charity.

Perhaps the most profound and useful verse for parents is Jesus's admonition, "For where your treasure is, there your heart will be also" (Matthew 6:21). This verse helps us to connect the dots for our children that all of our decisions with respect to money reflect our character and values as members of the body of Christ.

It's crucial in each circumstance that you weigh not only monetary considerations but also the principles that are reflected in every financial choice. For example, you may be able to afford a smartphone for your sixth grade son, but do you really want to put the power of the Internet into his hands without adequate supervision? And a Disney cruise may sound wonderful, but if you live a long distance from parents or other relatives, should you instead spend your money—and your time—visiting loved ones?

Of course, some things are conveniently overpriced. I would argue that anything they sell at Abercrombie and Fitch falls into this category, but perhaps I'm being a little strident. In any case, it's easy to use planning and spending decisions as teachable moments because explaining our decisions to our kids demonstrates our values in action.

Obviously, children want things, and it's often tough not to be able to give them the things they ask for. In our culture, children are programmed to be shoppers from an early age. Even before they can form full sentences, most toddlers can identify brands—to our parental astonishment. There's hardly a three-year-old in America who can't point to the golden arches from the back seat of the car and yell "McDonald's!" or to the Toys R Us logo and say "Toys!" Kudos to the folks on Madison Avenue for long ago discovering how to plant the seeds of consumerism in even the tiniest would-be shoppers, and then cultivating that specimen to maturity. This is why materialistic tweens have a taste for designer labels and personalized credit cards.

There was a time when children saved and earned their way to new things. However, between busy school, extracurricular, and sports schedules and the lack of opportunities for kids to earn money, the satisfaction of earning and saving their way to a big purchase is largely an accomplishment of the past.

Our materialistic culture also has created new habits for parents. We're only human, so the desire to keep up with the folks around us—and, in so doing, to make our children happy—is a natural one. And advertisers and marketers have done an exceptional job of convincing us that our kids *need* the very latest i-Everything or they'll be left out and behind the curve.

Being thusly persuaded, we're buying laptops for first graders on the belief that technology will be the path to learning, good grades, and future success; or worse, we're buying anything—from clothes to electronics to cars—on the belief that our purchases will facilitate our children's active and successful social lives. If we subscribe to the pressure to buy our kids' way into the cool crowd, we are sending them all the wrong messages about money, relationships, self-confidence, and character.

The teachable moment above poses an added consideration: the issue of comparing your family's financial status to that of your extended family and friends. This can be a source of envy, allowing money to poison relationships and foster poor character.

Moreover, children must learn that comparisons to others are never entirely accurate. Kids are quick to label their friends and family "lucky" for the things they have, so we must teach them that it takes hard work, sacrifices, and compromises to buy or do things in life.

The subject of money always allows us to infuse our conversations with value-laden messages about our priorities, beliefs, relationships, and character. Major themes you can discuss during these teachable moments include:

- *God asks us to steward our resources and make good decisions about money.* The way we live out our financial lives is woven into all the ways we express our faith as Christians. Having money is a huge responsibility, because it could easily pull us from a faithful walk with Jesus. When we use money for good, we're known as generous, charitable, caring, and compassionate.

- *Just because you can afford to do or buy something doesn't mean you should.* Decisions about spending must reflect what you value, not only what you can afford.

- *"Everyone else" isn't footing the bill.* Purchases and activities ought not be driven by what others are doing, but by your family's goals and priorities.

- *Financial limitations don't limit your ability to be content.* When we focus on contentment, life is satisfying even in the midst of financial ups and downs. Faith is free!

- *Comparison kills contentment.* Learning to be grateful for what we have, rather than comparing ourselves to others and focusing on what we don't have, is the path to genuine joy in life.

Teachable moments about money and financial issues give us the opportunity to promote in our children specific traits of good character, including:

- *Gratitude*—being thankful in all things. No matter what you give to or buy for your children, expect to be thanked. If you're not, remind them that gratitude is the awareness that everything that comes to us is a blessing.

- *Perseverance and patience*—working hard and saving for the future, and waiting patiently for the things we want. Even if you can give your children anything they want, create ways to make them earn or wait for things. The lessons learned in this process are invaluable.

- *Humility*—making do with the things we have and accepting that we can't always get what we want, when we want it. In a world where social status is often connected to materialism, kids must learn to put themselves, and not their stuff, foremost. Being stuck with an old-style phone, an off-brand of sneakers, or a rusty "beater" car can build character!

- *Frugality*—understanding the value of money and learning to use it wisely. The first lesson children need to learn about money is that it is a finite resource and must be managed appropriately. Rather than promote the fiction that there's an endless supply of funds, teach your child to compare the costs of things, to make smart purchasing decisions, and to look for good value in spending decisions.

- *Generosity*—sharing our blessings with others for the sheer joy of making others happy. Just as young children must be taught and reminded to share toys and turns, children must also be taught to share the blessings that money can bring.

- *Charity*—giving selflessly, not only from our excess but from our essence. Living gratefully and understanding that we are blessed means extending our blessings to those who are less fortunate. Teach your child that charity is the Christian response to others, and that money enables us to take care of those in need.

> The great danger for family life,
> in the midst of any society whose idols
> are pleasure, comfort, and independence,
> lies in the fact that people close their
> hearts and become selfish.
> —POPE ST. JOHN PAUL II

8. The moment: An older nephew has come out as gay. His mom, your sister-in-law, is proud of his courage for coming out and delighted that he is comfortable with his sexual orientation. She has made it a point to tell the family that he is in a committed relationship. She can't wait for him to bring his partner to upcoming holidays and family functions, and she hopes one day they'll get married. To that end, she's a vocal supporter of gay marriage.

As a Christian, you believe God calls us to love everyone, but that homosexual behavior is sinful. You're raising your kids in the church, where the teaching about this is clear. You love your nephew, and while you're fine with including his partner in social functions, you can't see your family attending a wedding of two men. It feels like you're being forced to accept the gay lifestyle in order to prove your love for a family member, and meanwhile, it's undermining what you are teaching your children about God's plan for human sexuality. How do you approach this complex and potentially difficult family issue?

The short answer: approach it lovingly. This is the most important way to be a Christian witness on the subject of homosexuality. Keep in mind that your sister-in-law is a mom who loves her son and wants him to be happy, so for her, embracing the political agenda of gay marriage is a way to outwardly demonstrate to her son that she loves and supports him.

As Christians, we're called to love everyone, but to reject sinfulness, even (and especially!) the sins that are made to seem harmless or even good for us. In our modern culture, "following your heart" has become the measure of morality. If your heart leads you to same-sex attraction, then by this definition it's "right."

Rational thinking sees the flaw in this argument. Your heart might lead you into the arms of a married neighbor, or into the back seat of car with your best friend's girlfriend, or into an affair with your pastor. The heart is a really unreliable guide for moral behavior. Morality, made clear to us by the teachings of Christ and supported by thousands of years of elaboration by the church, includes principles of right and wrong, good and bad, which are imprinted on our hearts in a code known as natural law. Morality isn't defined by what an individual thinks is okay, but by the architect of the universe itself.

God has not been vague about the morality surrounding human sexuality, and despite what popular culture would have everyone believe, Christianity still upholds this truth: the gift of sexuality is intended for one man and one woman in the context of a covenant marriage. That's the ideal. That's the goal. We humans fall short, but redefining the ideal doesn't make our alternatives right; it only makes us feel better about doing what's wrong.

So be assured that your Christian faith is guiding you to teach your children the truth about human sexuality. But Christianity is nothing if not challenging, right? Recall that Mahatma Gandhi said, "I like your Christ, I do not like your Christians. Your Christians are so unlike your Christ." If being Christlike were easy, everyone would do it!

The situation above calls you to be your most Christlike. Remember that Jesus ate with sinners of all stripes. He didn't condemn people, but rather loved them and made them want to follow him. But he also didn't shy away from speaking the truth in love. He IS the truth. He is love!

So, when your nephew brings his partner to family gatherings, treat his partner like a friend. Don't get caught up in conversations about their relationship, but rather get to know him as a person, aside from his being gay. Treat him just like you would any good friend that your nephew might bring to a family party.

If and when the subject of a gay wedding arises, you'll be faced with a prickly situation, to be sure. I've yet to hear of a circumstance when devoutly Christian family members have skipped a gay wedding and not paid for that decision with the anger of their relatives, but I believe it's the right thing to do. Your religious beliefs are meant to guide your life and actions. Respectfully declining an invitation to a gay wedding is fully consistent with your beliefs, as is lovingly accepting gay relatives for who they are.

How you turn this into a teachable moment for your children will vary depending on their ages. Our culture doesn't allow us to avoid the issue of homosexuality for even the youngest children (kindergarten literature now includes stories of families with gay couples), and TV shows and movies now casually portray gay characters even in content for children. It's likely children as young as seven years old might ask, "What does it mean to be gay?"

The rule of thumb when it comes to all kids' questions about sex and sexuality is to make sure you understand the context or origin of the question, and to give only as much information as you must give to satisfy your child's curiosity. You could answer, "Being gay is when two men or two women are attracted to each other romantically, the way God intends for men and women to be." As they get older, you must explain the difference between same-sex attraction—which is in itself not sinful, though we don't understand it—and sexual intimacy between members of the same sex, which is a sin.

Having a gay cousin means the lessons will be that much more personal for your kids. One way the gay agenda has become so widely accepted is that young people don't get why homosexuality is a big deal, and as they grow up with friends and family members who are gay, they are less likely to be concerned about it. This is why our teaching to young children on this issue must be biblically sound and crystal clear.

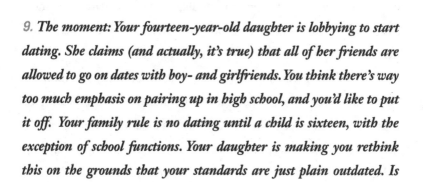

The right thing at the wrong time is the wrong thing.
—JOSHUA HARRIS

9. The moment: Your fourteen-year-old daughter is lobbying to start dating. She claims (and actually, it's true) that all of her friends are allowed to go on dates with boy- and girlfriends. You think there's way too much emphasis on pairing up in high school, and you'd like to put it off. Your family rule is no dating until a child is sixteen, with the exception of school functions. Your daughter is making you rethink this on the grounds that your standards are just plain outdated. Is fourteen old enough to date?

In a word: no. But in our culture, dating at fourteen—or younger!—is so commonplace as to be banal. If you've had a serious boyfriend since the sixth grade, why would you *not* go to the movies with him when you're a high school freshman? Sheesh!

These days, "dating" doesn't mean what we parents may think it means. Our kids don't "date" until they're already "going out," which is to say, they've declared their affection for each other (sometimes in person, sometimes by text, sometimes via a third party, but never by phone). If you've been "going out" for a while, you will eventually "date," perhaps by meeting at the movies or going out to eat in a group. You would also hang out exclusively at parties and you'd spend most of your "dating" life texting, chatting online, and declaring your feelings in social media.

It sounds innocent enough; sort of like passing notes in school, but digitally. Except when it's not.

Dating in adolescence introduces risks that outweigh the benefits. Some are big, such as sexual experimentation that can lead to serious physical and emotional consequences. But others—self-esteem issues, body image, and dating violence, to name only a few—are extremely difficult for teens to handle, much less share with their parents. Not to mention that old grade-killer, "boy-craziness," the nemesis of high school GPAs from coast to coast.

The role of parents in this situation is to set limits and monitor your child's behavior as she matures naturally, with the passing of time. However, it feels like we're always in a battle to hold back the floodgates of social acceleration. Our culture wants to grow kids up at lightning speed, moving them from "tween" to "young adult" with nary a moment to stew in an old-fashioned episode of teenage angst. Making your child wait until later to start dating—say, sixteen or seventeen—is one way of assuring that she has had time to gain self-confidence and social skills before adding romance to her list of concerns.

Of course, this won't seem fair to a fourteen-year-old. When situations like this arise, turn them into teachable moments about dating and socializing by focusing on your concerns, as well as the benefits of a positive social life. You might explain it like this: "We get that almost everyone you know is allowed to date and to be in an exclusive relationship, but we're certain you're too young for that kind of relationship. There can be a lot of pressure to do things you don't want to do, and to act in ways that make you feel bad about yourself just so you can please a guy. It may seem like you want a boyfriend or you want to start dating, but romantic relationships at your age get complicated and hurtful really easily. We'd rather that you're free to be yourself, because having a boyfriend at your age can take the fun out of being fourteen."

You also will want to teach your daughter that being honest and transparent will enable you to facilitate a fun social life for her. Remind her of this by saying, "We want you to have a lot of friends and a fun, busy social life, and we're fine with group activities where kids aren't paired off. The best way for you to have a good social life is to be transparent with us, so that we feel comfortable letting you do things with your friends. If you're not always straight with us about what's going on and who you're with, we'll have to pull the reins in tighter until we can trust you to be honest with us. This is where your good character and your reputation for integrity are so important. You'll benefit when you show us that you have strong character."

Exhibiting good character and enjoying the privileges that result from it is a lot more fun than having a boyfriend, as anyone who has ever had a fourteen-year-old boyfriend will attest!

> I didn't want to be like everyone else.
> I wanted to be better.
> If I did what everybody else did,
> then why would you look up to me?
> Why would I set an example?
>
> —TIM TEBOW

10. The moment: You're worried your middle schooler is too cool. She was always a popular and friendly girl throughout elementary school. Now that she's in middle school, she is in the "cool" group of girls who wear the latest styles, are experts at putting on makeup, and even wear high heels to school. It bothers you that she and her friends are too sexy for their age.

Not only is her attire an issue but her Facebook and Twitter pages have lots of "duck-face selfies"—those pictures where the girls pucker their lips and try to look alluring in the mirror. The messages she and her friends post online are constantly referring to people as "sexy" and "hot."

Your daughter insists that her behavior is appropriate. She swears she's not dating or "hooking up" with guys, so you shouldn't be concerned about the way she dresses. She is just fitting in with her friends. It feels like you're losing the war against the hypersexual culture, one tacky, low-cut T-shirt at a time. What can you do?

Adolescence is uncomfortable for everyone, isn't it? One day you're happily chugging along, enjoying the delightful antics of your ten-year-old daughter, and the next, puberty moves in like an unwelcome houseguest, flooding the basement with a deluge of inexplicable tears, fickle emotions, and awkward lunges toward sexual identity. And those are the good days!

On the bad days, you're trying to explain to a thirteen-year-old that skanky and sexy are two different things, neither of which is appropriate for the attire of a wholesome middle schooler. Sadly, the culture in which kids are immersed makes it difficult for them to ignore the hypersexual messages that bombard them every day. From the songs they sing in the shower to the Web sites they visit to shop for clothes (beware—Abercrombie's site is legitimate soft-core porn!), our adolescent children are being taught that growing up means looking, acting, and thinking "sexy."

So in that sense, who could blame a cool, popular daughter for keeping up with her friends when she transitions from girlhood to adolescence? In today's culture, the behavior she's exhibiting is not just common, it's considered normal.

Unfortunately, it's more than tacky: it can be downright dangerous. Girls don't seem to appreciate that their pouty "selfies" and busty bathing suit pics aren't just imitations of their favorite pop stars. They are tacitly advertising that their sexuality defines who they are and what they're interested in, even if they aren't acting on these urges with a boyfriend.

For today's Christian parents, the hyper-sexualizing of American adolescence should be a "hill to die on." Sexuality is a defining issue in the maturation process, so parents who let the culture indoctrinate their children on the topic of sex are implicitly nodding approval for sexual activity in adolescence. If you want your children to remain abstinent in adolescence and chaste until marriage, you have to draw a direct connection between the "sexy persona" and the behavior it ultimately promotes.

The Lesson Plan

Let's remember what the role of a parent is really all about—participating in God's creation by stewarding the children he has given us and rearing them for heaven (not for Harvard!). All the success and popularity and "happiness" in the world won't replace the genuine joy your children will experience because of a strong character and a virtuous life. The number one thing to do is to keep your focus on what's truly important for your children's future.

Here is a summary of the basics you need to focus on:

- *Teach moral lessons at every age* and in every stage of childhood, expecting that your children are capable of understanding morality and acting on their consciences.

- *Expect obedience,* don't just ask for cooperation.

- *Choose more battles* and infuse them with character-building lessons.

- *Parent intentionally, according to your values,* not simply by accepting what everyone else is doing as suitable for your family.

- *Look for teachable moments* within your daily home life to instill character, conscience, and faith.

CHAPTER THREE

Teachable Media Moments

A TRUISM ABOUT MEDIA IS: it's everywhere we go, and it's not going anywhere. Such is the culture in which we live. Sometimes we have to make the effort *not* to engage with media.

Every so often our family's consumption of media has felt excessive, and I've declared a moratorium. When my children were little, I easily accomplished this with a dramatic wave of the TV remote while pronouncing, "Everybody outside!" Now that the "kids" are young adults, it's more likely that we agree to leave our smartphones behind while walking the dog, or spend an evening in our living room, where there's no TV.

It's easy to blame our media for all of the social and cultural ills around us. Heck, who couldn't look to someone like Miley Cyrus, a talented girl raised in a Christian home, and decide that our exploitative, hypersexual media is literally stealing children out from under our noses? Stories about cyberbullying, video game addiction, pornography addiction, and media obsessions give evidence that media is being used effectively by the Evil One.

Still, it's important to remember that technology in itself is morally neutral. Just as it can be used to compromise or even corrupt our children's souls, it also can be a tool to teach and promote the lessons they need to live moral and faithful lives. Media devices, if used in a positive way, can bring us together rather than isolate us from each other. The trick is to have mastery over our media consumption, and not let media have mastery over us.

Like so many things, our use of media often becomes unintentional. There probably isn't a parent in America who'd say it's okay that their kids spend every waking hour engaged with media, but most folks don't think twice about letting kids watch TV or play a video game until dinner, or pop in their ear buds while doing homework, or press "play" on the video player in the van on the way to the orthodontist. Often it's easier, and more convenient, to say yes to media than to face the inevitable hassle and resistance that follows when we say no. At the same time, the ubiquitous nature of our media makes it nearly impossible to monitor or control all of the content to which our children are exposed. Rather than evaluate content for ourselves, we end up trusting ratings systems, familiar entertainment companies, or networks that sound family-friendly to choose content for us.

Just when you think you're adequately supervising the media that comes into your home, you discover that certain shows on a network that includes the word "family" in its name are about as wholesome as a college spring break on the beach. As Christians, we're called to integrate our media consumption into our lives in ways that support our faith and values, and not as a perpetual temptation or an avenue of corruption. But this is easier said than done.

How do you handle Facebook posts from friends that link to offensive music videos featuring graphic lyrics about sex and drugs? What about commercials for birth control that imply all single women are having premarital sex? Or video games that seem mostly okay, but include graphic violence and morally ambiguous narratives? What about TV dramas that make people of faith seem hokey or judgmental?

And it's not just entertainment content that may hijack your efforts to protect your children's innocence. One errant click of a computer mouse and your children may find themselves on a Web site that shocks and confuses them. A simple search for information about a school project can expose a child to truly vile content.

Using Media Intentionally

These realities are why it's crucial that we are intentional about our use of media. Three basic principles ought to guide and direct media consumption:

1. *Media content ought to reflect your values.* The messages that media content brings to your hearts and minds ought to be consistent with what you believe to be good and right. To live authentically according to the beliefs that guide you, you have to resist the desensitizing that happens when you ignore unaccept-

able media content. Instead, reconnect with a sense of righteous indignation; remember what it feels like to be offended, and model good habits of media consumption and content selection.

2. *Media consumption ought to promote—not erode—our wholeness.* A whole person doesn't do just one thing. People who engage with media for a majority of their free time (not to mention for professional or educational purposes) aren't feeding the rest of their mind, body, heart, and spirit. If you're worried that you or your children spend too much time with media, you or they probably do.

3. *Media literacy protects your family.* You can't teach your children why media content is inappropriate—or even evil—if you don't know how to assess it properly. In the same way, you need to be able to tell your kids why other media choices are wholesome and healthy. Learning how to deconstruct media content and put it in the context of its intended messages gives you the knowledge you need to take advantage of teachable media moments.

The Center for Media Literacy advises that parents can nurture media literacy in their children by helping them master the following concepts:

- *Media messages are constructed.* Kids need to learn that the messages being communicated in media aren't there by accident; they're deliberately constructed and intended to be understood and acted upon. When a child knows all media has a message, that child is more likely to find the message.

- *Messages are representations of reality with embedded values and points of view.* Even in a cartoon story, all media content stands for something. There's no such thing as value-less media; our kids need to learn the skill of discerning the values contained within the stories, songs, ads, and so on.

  Each form of media relies on unique techniques such as sound, visual effects, lighting, point of view, and voice in order to construct messages. These elements help convey the intended meaning of media content. Kids can learn to appreciate the nuances of various forms of media content. By dissecting the production of media content, we can teach them to find the underlying meaning and values being communicated. For example, bad guys tend to wear dark colors and are unattractive, whereas good guys tend to be brighter and more appealing.

- *People interpret media messages and create their own meaning based on personal experience.* We all view media through the prism of our opinions, beliefs, and values, and kids are no different, except that they have less life experience on which to assess what they see. This means they're more prone to believe whatever they're told through the media and less able to assess the validity or truth of a message.

- *Media are driven by profit within economic and political contexts.* Kids can understand that someone is usually making money where media messages are concerned. They will learn to be wary of media content, especially advertising, if they learn how to "follow the money" and find who profits by shaping the consumer's behavior and opinions.

Kids can't unsee what they've seen. They won't forget the catchy tune with the lyrics about "molly" (thanks for that ecstasy reference, Miley Cyrus . . . not). They won't unhear the use of the n-word by popular rappers, or a hit sitcom's references to threesomes. But neither will they forget the powerful messages in the positive content they will encounter, such as the compelling stories of faith and courage found in documentaries and movies such as *The Way*. There is much to be found in media that uplifts us, which we can use to teach our children positive lessons. We parents can impart influential life lessons when we look for teachable moments in and around our use of media.

Ten Teachable Media Moments

I didn't know what Facebook was, and now that I do know what it is, I have to say, it sounds like a huge waste of time.

—BETTY WHITE

1. The moment: Your twelve-year-old daughter wants to get a Facebook page. You're aware that Facebook's policy is that users must be thirteen or older, but almost all of your child's friends are already on the social media site. What's more, they all use Twitter, ask.fm, Instagram, Snapchat, and Vine. You're not even sure what all of these social sites do, much less whether you should allow your child to join them. What's the right age to allow social media? Are these sites okay for tweens and teens?

While Facebook allows users thirteen years and older, I would argue that most thirteen-year-olds lack the social skills and judgment for social media, and that anyone younger than high school is not ready to be on Facebook, Twitter, Instagram, SnapChat, Vine or other sites. There are too many opportunities to make mistakes, many of which can be serious and have lasting effects.

By now, we're all aware of the cyberbullying that has torn apart school communities and even resulted in suicides due to acute depression on the part of victims of bullying. Technology allows kids to spread horrible rumors and levy harmful insults while hiding behind the veil of a virtual persona. Because of the enormous power of the Internet, a child's reputation and self-esteem can be destroyed with the click of a cyberbully's mouse.

But it's not just the risk of cyberbullying or meeting strangers online or even becoming addicted to social media (that's a thing!) that concerns me most. It's the fact that parents too often allow peer pressure to dictate their decisions about letting kids join social media. I can't count the number of parents who've told me, "I hate that my child is on Twitter all the time, but everyone else is doing it, so I guess it's okay," or, "I don't like Instagram for my middle schooler, but having my child excluded from her social life would be worse." My response to these folks is, "Just to be clear, you're telling me Instagram does not reflect your values about media for your child, but you're allowing it anyway." I always smile when I say this because otherwise I would seem really snarky.

Both age and maturity should drive the decision to let kids join social networking sites. Just because a child is older than thirteen doesn't mean that child is ready to use social media, much of which feeds teenagers' propensity for impulsivity. If you affirmatively believe social media is not in your child's best interest, you have to say no. Period. And then you have to supervise your child to assure that your decision is respected.

I didn't say this would be easy.

Let's say you are considering allowing your daughter to use social media. This decision is a great teachable moment. Together with your child, look at her life through a wide lens so she can see how to integrate social media in a healthy manner. Is she involved in a variety of activities, including sports, hobbies, and clubs at school, or, if she's old enough, a part-time job? If there's not enough on her plate to keep her busy, social media could become her primary pastime (again, social network addiction is real). That obviously wouldn't be healthy.

Assess your child's academic performance and work habits. Is she serious and dedicated enough as a student to withstand the distraction of Facebook or Twitter? These sites can tempt a great student to slip into procrastination and wasting time.

Make an honest assessment of your child's maturity level. Is she impulsive? Does she tend to gossip? Do her peers sometimes misunderstand her humor? Does she try too hard to be accepted by the popular kids? All of these would certainly be amplified by using social media.

If you go forward with the decision to allow social media, make it subject to your ongoing supervision. Be informed and engaged; you have to know what the various platforms are and how they work. And retreat when necessary! Anytime you see your child use social media as a tool for unkind or immoral behavior, or it becomes all-consuming, you're obligated to pull the plug.

When kids say "everyone is using social media," they're not kidding. Pope Francis is our *second* pontiff tweeting (as @Pontifex)! As parents, our job is to introduce this technology into our children's lives at an appropriate time, assuring that they've had the chance to grow up in the real world before they stumble unprepared through cyberspace.

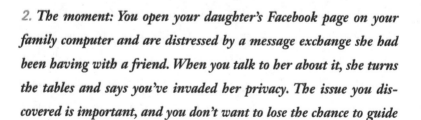

If you have something that you don't want anyone to know, maybe you shouldn't be doing it in the first place.

—ERIC SCHMIDT, CEO OF GOOGLE

2. The moment: You open your daughter's Facebook page on your family computer and are distressed by a message exchange she had been having with a friend. When you talk to her about it, she turns the tables and says you've invaded her privacy. The issue you discovered is important, and you don't want to lose the chance to guide your daughter's behavior, but now you're only arguing about privacy and whether you trust her. How much privacy should you allow your daughter in cyberspace?

How much privacy you allow depends on the child and the record of trust she has built. But to be clear, your minor child's privacy in cyberspace (or any space, for that matter) is not an entitlement. Our obligation and responsibility to rear our children means we have the right to know what's going on. That's the only way we can guide and teach them.

Beyond that general principal about transparency, Rule No. 1 for social networking is: there's no such thing as privacy. The message exchange you read may have been intended for your daughter and her friend, but the friend could easily have taken a screen shot of that message and sent it elsewhere. It's critical that kids understand that technology can be manipulated by anyone who wants to violate their intended privacy.

As for you reading her message exchange, the approach you take depends on the situation. If you read it because you were suspicious that something was up, say so. If you read it out of curiosity, admit you weren't worried, you just wanted a glimpse into her friendship. In any case, your child needs to know the bottom line: "I'm your mom, and I have an obligation to rear you as God has called me to do. What you call invading your privacy, I call parenting."

Kids are quick to back their parents into a corner with the accusation, "You don't trust me!" as though the parent is bound to prove that they do. Don't fall for it! In our house, the answer is, "Of course I do! I trust you to be a teenager who will sometimes make mistakes." Trust is earned and rewarded with confidence, responsibility, and yes—privacy. But it's not an entitlement until our children are on their own and living as independent adults.

> ## We played the game by day and lived the game by night.
>
> **—AN ANONYMOUS, INCARCERATED OAKLAND, CALIFORNIA, GANG MEMBER TALKING ABOUT THE GAME GRAND THEFT AUTO**

3. *The moment: Your son wants to play the same video games as his friends, but the games they play are violent. He's fifteen and says you're too strict about this issue; he's not going to become a deranged killer by playing war games. Are violent video games really a problem?*

Actually, violent video games *are* a problem, especially for younger children, and unfortunately, violence in games is more prevalent than parents may think. A 2011 study from Simmons College found 71 percent of video games contained at least some mild violence, while 25 percent included intense violence, blood, and gore. In fact, research shows that children ages seven to twelve routinely play games rated M for mature audiences—the most violent and graphic kind.

Violent video games can be addictive, as players experience the "thrill of the kill" and seek to feed the emotional response that these games stimulate. Studies indicate that teenage boys are especially susceptible to gaming addiction because of the way their brains respond. This is the real danger of violent video games, more so than that they lead to violent criminal activity. Parents ought also to be concerned about the impact of video games on a child's character and conscience. The combination of realistic graphics and narratives that allow players to explore evil fantasies, vicariously perpetrating acts of aggression, violence, and death, creates a morally compromising experience. Even if the player isn't really "doing" the action, the emotional and psychological sensations are real. Ultimately, they desensitize the player to violent acts.

In fact, the Simmons study proved that violent games impact a child's moral reasoning, teaching kids that violence is acceptable and sometimes the best response. Moral reasoning is based on understanding the perspectives of others, but violent video games provide no perspective on the suffering of victims, and actually impede this crucial developmental step.

If your fifteen-year-old son has had time to develop a conscience and a sense of morality about violence, you may think he's past the point of being influenced by graphically violent games. But even if he is, the fundamental issue about media consumption remains: does the content reflect your values?

Which is not to say that this point will convince your son. After all, as he notes, his buddies play these games, and they aren't bad kids. Such a response presents an opportunity for a teachable moment about moral consistency. Ask your son, "How would you feel if I got involved in an online dating environment and fantasized about having an affair? It's not that I'd actually do it; I'd just enjoy the excitement of imagining it. Would that be a wholesome way to spend my time?" This kind of comparison might help him understand that seeking out immoral thoughts and feelings has a consequence to his heart and soul, even if he doesn't act on them in "real life."

> **Make no mistake,
> I am a Christian and I believe in God
> and I don't believe he makes mistakes,
> so I believe that being gay is not a sin
> and in fact it's how you're made.**
>
> —KRISTIN CHENOWETH

4. The moment: Television content seems determined to promote the normalizing of homosexuality and transgenderism. From television series such as **Glee,** *which portray gay teens in a positive and moral light, to documentaries about small children who undergo transgender therapy, media content about sex and sexuality undermines your Christian beliefs. How can you combat this one-sided portrayal in the media?*

By now we're all accustomed to the fact that Hollywood, and the vast majority of people who work in media, believe that homosexuality is not sinful and that what we might refer to as a "gay agenda" should be the cultural norm. Thanks in large measure to the manner in which homosexuality has been portrayed in the media, Americans are changing their belief about the sin of homosexual behavior.

To wit: a 2013 story in *USA Today* carried this headline: "Survey: Big Drop in Those Who Say Being Gay's a Sin." According to Life-Way Research, a division of LifeWay Christian Resources of the Southern Baptist Convention, significantly fewer Americans defined homosexual behavior as sinful in 2012 than in 2011.

As reported at LifeWay.com:

A November 2012 survey of adults in the United States found 37 percent affirm a belief that homosexual behavior is a sin—a statistically significant change from a September 2011 LifeWay Research survey asking the same question. At that time, 44 percent answered "Yes."

Statistics among young people show even greater numbers who believe that being gay is not sinful, and that sexual relationships among gays are natural and normal.

Television shows such as *Glee* (not to mention virtually everything that airs on MTV) have had a huge impact on the opinions and attitudes of young people, so parents should use them for important teachable moments. This doesn't mean you should let your kids watch these shows! Usually, the teaching comes in explaining why you *don't* approve of certain TV shows, movies, songs, and so on. The trick is, to impart the lesson you can't just say no. You have to say, "No, and this is why . . ."

Here's where those skills of media literacy and a solid understanding of Christian teachings combine to help parents create a crucial lesson for their kids. The Center for Media Literacy has defined five key questions for analyzing media:

1. Who created this message?

2. What creative techniques are used to attract my attention?

3. How might different people understand this message differently from me?

4. What lifestyles, values, and points of view are represented in, or omitted from, this message?

5. Why is this message being sent?

It doesn't take much googling to find the answers to these five questions about any media content that concerns or interests you.

Using these questions, you might deconstruct *Glee* for your kids by saying something like this: "The show's creator is Ryan Murphy, a talented and successful writer and director who is also a gay activist. Murphy was raised in the church and went to Catholic schools, but has rejected Christian teachings about homosexuality. He uses a cast of appealing and wildly talented young actors who sing and act their way through a fictional high school while telling sympathetic stories that convey Murphy's beliefs about a number of topics, including sex, sexuality, and religion. Folks who agree with Murphy's agenda would understand the messages in the show to be affirming. But Christians see the messages in the show as an effort to normalize behaviors that are contrary to God's natural law and to our faith. Generally, Murphy doesn't depict religious people sympathetically, but rather portrays them as judgmental and bigoted. He's sending this message because he wants to teach kids his worldview; he wants to influence his audience's opinions and beliefs. He also wants to produce a successful show and make money, as all TV producers want to do."

Media content about transgenderism seeks to convey the people who seek sex reassignment as sympathetic and reasoned in their pursuit of an alternative identity. The incidence of transgenderism as a medical disorder among our population remains infinitesimally small—0.1 to 0.5 percent of the total population, according to a report from the Los Angeles County Department of Public Health—and is exceedingly rare among children. Other than the extremely small number of people who suffer from the medical disorder known as gender dysphoria, transgenderism is part of the continuum of sexual deviancy that many folks are trying to normalize.

When children are exposed to information about transgenderism, parents can use this as a teachable moment about how we can't let the culture convince us of things that aren't true. You could say something like, "In very rare cases, there is a medical reason why someone might experience gender confusion. Most of the time, people need support and prayers so that they can accept their bodies lovingly from God."

The most effective way to prevent this kind of content from influencing your child's opinions is to reject it because it seeks to undermine your Christian values. But the point is, if you want to instill your values, it's not enough to only reject certain content. You must also teach your kids why you object to it.

Whoever controls the media controls the mind.
—JIM MORRISON

5. *The moment: While watching TV one evening during the "family hour," you tune into what appears to be a suitable situation comedy. The next thing you know, the characters are discussing "threesomes." The show is on for several seconds before you can grab*

the remote and change the channel. You explain away your response by saying the show was rude. Should you sit your kids down and tell them what that was about, and why you reacted as you did?

When you consider the manner in which sex is portrayed in the media—and especially married sex, as compared to adulterous or premarital sex—it's easy to wonder whether our children's generation will ever understand what a constitutes a "healthy marriage." On television, married couples are portrayed as disinterested and asexual, while couples engaged in kinky, taboo, or illicit sexual relationships are depicted as more appealing, attractive and "sexy."

If you're shocked by what you see on television, even during the so-called family hour, one study proves you are hardly a prude. In 2008, the Parents Television Council published an important study entitled "Happily Never After: How Hollywood Favors Adultery and Promiscuity Over Marital Intimacy on Prime Time Broadcast Television," which quantified the degree to which sex outside of marriage, including scandalous behaviors, is celebrated, while marital sex is seen as confining and "unsexy."

Some of the study's key findings, found at ParentsTV.org, explain why parents struggle to safeguard their kids from inappropriate sexual content on TV:

- Across the broadcast networks, verbal references to non-marital sex outnumbered references to sex in the context of marriage by nearly three to one, and scenes depicting or implying sex between nonmarried partners outnumbered scenes depicting or implying sex between married partners by a ratio of nearly four to one.

- References to adultery outnumbered references to marital sex two to one.

- Although the networks shied away from talking about sex in the context of marriage, they did not shy away from discussions of masturbation, oral sex, anal sex, manual stimulation, sex toys, bondage, or kinky or fetishistic sex—there were seventy-four such references during the study period.

- The Family Hour—the time slot with the largest audience of young viewers where one might reasonably expect broadcasters to be more careful with the messages they are communicating to impressionable youngsters—contained the highest frequency of references to nonmarried sex. Family Hour references to nonmarital sex outnumbered references to sex in marriage by a ratio of 3.9 to 1.

Clearly, the likelihood that kids will be exposed to sexual content that conflicts with your values and religious beliefs is approximately 100 percent, so prepare that ready answer!

How to revisit sexual content on TV depends on your children. If your child comes to you with a direct question, tell the truth. Keep in mind that you can protect your children's innocence even as you share information. Ignorance and innocence are not the same things; it all depends on context.

Say your daughter comes to you and says, "Hey, you and dad reacted really oddly to that show the other night. What's a 'threesome,' anyway?" Here's how you might answer (right after you stall for time, sip your coffee, and invite the Holy Spirit to help you!): "The word itself just means 'three people,' but the show we were watching meant it as a sexual reference, implying three people in a sexual situation. Obviously, that's not God's plan for the gift of human sexuality, so we turned it off. Unfortunately, it's hard to find TV shows that don't make those kinds of jokes about sex, but they're always inappropriate."

Out of curiosity, some kids might ask how that sort of thing would work. Your answer? "I have absolutely no idea. I don't even think about things like that."

If your child doesn't ask you about it but you'd like to follow up—and assuming you've already given her age-appropriate information about sex—you could say something like, "By the way, the other night we were pretty sure that show was talking about an inappropriate, unholy sexual theme, and we weren't going to hang around to find out!"

The saturation of sexual references throughout entertainment media, but especially on television, requires you to have open and informative conversations with your children about sex and sexuality. It is impossible to compete with the values of our hypersexual culture unless you speak frankly and comfortably about the manner in which sex is portrayed in the media. The upside? Those kinds of conversations are best for kids because they allow you to instill your values on this most essential topic.

We spend too much time fretting over
the way the industry produces programming,
and too little worrying about the way
the public consumes it.

—MICHAEL MEDVED

*6. The moment: You're in a constant battle with your tween daughter
about the TV shows she wants to watch. You think the programming
on MTV and other popular networks like it is inappropriate, but
you're worried that if you ban them, she'll watch them behind your
back (online or at a friend's house, for example). How do you limit
your daughter's media access without driving her underground?*

This is a tough issue. Kids want to feel included, to participate in
the conversations that take place at the lunch table at school, for example. Often, those revolve around the latest TV shows, music videos,
songs, movies, and so on. No parent wants his or her child to feel left
out, but that's a bad reason for allowing your daughter's innocence to
be corrupted! So, what do you do? Tell her, "No, honey, because that
show is not good enough for your beautiful, sweet heart and soul."

If she's old enough to want to watch media content that troubles
you, she's old enough for a frank conversation about media and your
values. Don't have this conversation when she asks you if she can
watch a particular show, but rather make it a more formal, thoughtful discussion. First, do your research so you can speak knowledge-
ably about the media in question. Then open the conversation with
something like this:

"Honey, I know you want to watch (insert name of objectionable show here), and I get that your friends are allowed to watch this show, but here's the problem I have. That program conflicts with our values. I watched a few episodes and I didn't like the language, or the way they referred casually to sexual situations, or (add more specific nasty stuff here). It's not that I am trying to spoil your fun, I just can't allow that show to spoil your heart."

Eventually, after you have this talk about several shows, you can simply say, "That's another show that just isn't good enough for you."

Now for the hard part: How do you keep your daughter from going behind your back or seeing objectionable media at friends' houses? Unless you're going to follow her everywhere she goes or wire your house with closed-circuit cameras, the short answer is: you can't. Kids will be sneaky and disobey you, and this behavior is called sin. It's pretty much a given in the human experience.

However, if you're doing your job, she should feel guilty about it. Developing her conscience is a big part of your to-do list on God's behalf. Eventually, as you instill your values and develop your child's moral character, she will make discerning choices about her media consumption.

If you discover she has seen a show or movie that you've banned, deal with the issue of disobedience, but don't miss the teachable moment about media content. Keep in mind that it's often difficult for kids to censor the media choices of their friends, even if they want to. The important thing is to keep the lines of communication open so your daughter tells you about the media to which she's exposed. That's the only way you can put it in the context of your faith and values.

> Purity prepares the soul for love,
> and love confirms the soul in purity.
> —JOHN HENRY CARDINAL NEWMAN

7. The moment: Your son stays overnight at the home of a friend, a good kid who has a history of minor misbehavior. You ask how the night was and your son says it was fine, but he's acting a little oddly. Within a week of the sleepover, you notice he's clicking out of Web sites whenever you walk toward the home office, and the browser history is always cleared. You're worried he is getting into Internet porn, but you don't know for sure, and you don't want to embarrass him.

Whether or not you can confirm that your son is viewing pornography online, this is a conversation that must be had with every boy in America. The overnight stay and your suspicions are enough to create a teachable moment about the dangers of Internet porn, regardless of whether you catch your son looking at such sites.

Too many parents ignore this issue because, let's face it, it's embarrassing to try and engage a teen or preteen boy in a conversation about pornography. Still, without guidance from parents and a strong household policy about Internet porn, boys can fall into porn and masturbation addictions quickly, with devastating consequences.

Research now proves that porn and sex addictions work the same way in the brain as addictions to drugs and alcohol. In order to maintain a level of stimulation, more and more of the substance must be consumed. In the case of pornography, the stimulus must become more graphic and violent, and with sex addiction, the quantity of sexual encounters becomes all consuming.

Worse, pornography use among young men is creating high levels of sexual dysfunction, meaning they are unable to become sexually aroused by normal affection and intimacy. With the consequences of porn and sex addiction so great, it is imperative that parents use the teachable moments of Internet use to broach this difficult subject.

Anytime a child clicks out of a Web site in order to hide it from you, you have reason to suspect something. Clearing the Internet history is a telltale sign that a child is visiting inappropriate Web sites. But kids have far more Internet access than simply through the family computer—any kid with an i-Anything can get online to view pornography. (This is why the iPod Touch is often referred to as the iPorn, because it allows access to the net without parental supervision.)

At the outset of this chapter, I reminded you that media is everywhere and is not going anywhere. This means that regular, frank conversations about the use and dangers of pornography are essential to assure the safety and health of our young boys and men.

To be fair, this is also, sadly, a growing issue among girls. Everyone who uses the Internet needs to understand the ramifications of pornography.

Finally, it's important to convey your concerns about porn use not only in terms of the sexual sins it promotes but also the sin of exploitation of others. When we objectify other human beings, we degrade them and rob them of their human dignity—even if they willingly cooperated in the making of a pornographic video. As Christians, we are obliged to reject pornography not only because it degrades our souls but also because it dehumanizes other human beings.

> **Kids need to remember
> that when you put something on Twitter,
> it's not like whispering to your friend—
> you've put it on a billboard that the whole world,
> including your own kids someday, can see.**
> —BILL COSBY

8. The moment: You go online to check out your daughter's Twitter feed. Clicking through a few tweets from people you don't recognize, you discover that there is a party being planned for the weekend that is clearly going to include drinking, drugs, and hooking up. The tweets indicate that the host family obviously has no idea what is being planned. You decree that your child will not attend the party, but you wonder if you should report your findings to the host family.

This question is an example of me talking to myself. This really happened; it's not hypothetical. It's happening to parents all across our country on any given weekend, so it's an issue that must be addressed.

Social media may seem like the bane of our parental existences, because if we're acting responsibly as parents, we're monitoring our children's social media use. File this task under "Things I Didn't Want to Make Time For." But as a social-media-savvy mom, I'm more inclined to think these sites are gold mines of information—especially Twitter. Most kids do not protect their Twitter feeds, meaning anyone on Twitter can read their posts. This may sound dangerous, but in reality, I think it's a blessing for those of us parents who want real information about what our teenagers are exposed to.

Here's how it worked for me. My daughter mentioned that a guy friend she had known since grade school was having a house party. He was co-hosting the party at his home with friends of his from other schools, and they planned to invite kids from all over our community. His parents planned to be at home and supposedly were prepared to supervise.

I almost never say yes to a party of this sort (and by "almost never" I mean "never"), but my daughter insisted that my concerns were unfounded. The party would be supervised! The parents would be there! What could possibly go wrong?

I took to Twitter to find out. What I learned was that the host parents had no idea that their son's co-hosts were turning their social gathering into an "epic" event. One of the teens involved posted links to the anonymous question-and-answer site ask.fm (a free site that lets users respond to anonymously posed questions), where information was disseminated on how to sneak alcohol into the bash, how to be cool if you're using drugs, and who planned to hook up with whom.

I was scandalized by the information I discovered, and that's saying a lot coming from a culture columnist. I'm not easily shocked.

What to do with this information? First, I reaffirmed that my daughter would in no way be attending this event, epic or not.

In the week before the party, I spoke to every parent I saw at school events. I asked if they were letting their kids go to the party, and if they were, explained how to view the information I had seen online. (I was not the most popular mom in the village when a few kids ended up being banned from the bash.)

Finally, I made sure the school was aware of what I'd seen, so that they could approach the family whose home was about to be turned into a teenage crime scene. The administration already knew about it, and they had been in contact with the family. My mission was complete.

I didn't go directly to the host family because I didn't know them. I also guessed they would be defensive about whether they were doing something wrong, and I didn't want to put my daughter in the middle of my vigilantism. So I did what I could in my circle of influence.

Most importantly, I made sure my daughter knew exactly what I was doing and why. We sat down together and read the Twitter and ask.fm feeds, talking through the various comments and statements, as well as the potential dangers they implied. (If you don't know what ask.fm is, you need to educate yourself. It's uniquely despicable among social media sites because it relies on anonymity.)

On the night of that party, my daughter hung out in our family room. The Instagram photos alone were proof enough the parents could not have been supervising what was going on. With teens overrunning the property inside and out, they'd have needed a staff of security guards to know what was really happening.

The week of that party offered several memorable teachable moments, including my willingness to use whatever means were available to parent my daughter effectively. We can't afford to be uninvolved in social media if we want to know what's going on in our children's universe. The information there could literally save lives, and certainly prevent a world of hurt.

> This will be our reply to violence:
> to make music more intensely,
> more beautifully, more devotedly
> than ever before.
> —LEONARD BERNSTEIN

9. The moment: You pop your head into your son's room to check on him while he's doing his homework. He's diligently working on sixth grade math while nodding his head to the beat of a song on his headphones. You interrupt him to see how it's going, and decide impulsively to pop on his Beats to check out his playlist. What you hear is shocking. Vile, vulgarity-filled rap music assaults your senses. You're stunned! Do you take away your son's headphones? Shut down his iTunes account? How do you control this sort of music in your home?

The good news: You're still capable of being shocked. The bad news: Your sixth grader's innocence has certainly been corrupted by Kendrick Lamar, Drake, and 2 Chainz.

Popular music is an area in which parents are able to take very little control, thanks in part to the "sanitized" versions of songs that air on regular radio stations, but leave little to the imagination when it comes to vulgarity and inappropriate content. Add to this the ease and convenience of using sites such as Spotify and Pandora, and you can't even monitor your children's musical choices by virtue of approving download purchases, because they can listen to anything they want to hear using these free music sites. And really, why own music when you can listen to anything you want, any time you want, for free?

There are three things you can do, however, if you're willing to put in the time and effort:

First, have standards in your home about the music you allow, in the same way you need standards for television shows, movies, Internet sites, and other forms of media. Your standards might include specific language or themes you won't permit, music video content you won't allow, or specific artists or genres you choose to ban from your home.

Second, sit down with your son and explain why you are setting these standards. Broadly, it's the same reason as always: media must reflect the values you hold in your home. Specifically, musical themes may not degrade women, glamorize drugs and violence, promote "thug" culture and disrespect for authority, or focus far too much on sex as the center of relationships.

Finally, listen to the music your kids listen to, at least sometimes. Putting on the headphones is an essential exercise because otherwise we allow our kids to consume media content in isolation. Only by listening to their music do we get the chance to impose our values on their choices and teach the lessons they must learn about the implications of media content.

Music is a powerful tool to engage the heart and mind. An American Academy of Pediatrics study indicates that adolescents who listen to sexually explicit lyrics are more likely to engage in precocious sexual activity than those who don't. And there is no denying that music stirs thoughts and feelings in teens that can be destructive and self-destructive.

There are those who dismiss concerns about music content on the grounds that every generation has its musical soundtrack, and every generation of parents objects to it. This line of thinking is a cop-out for avoiding an uncomfortable reality: popular music may be responsible for a certain devolution of our culture. (Some have credited it for bringing back the n-word, which had been successfully banned until its use was resurrected in rap and hip-hop music).

Music is also an area that can bring families together. Mine has rallied around country music (not always an innocent choice either, but at least it's generally patriotic and respectful). Even so, when it comes to monitoring musical choices, "Turn that off!" is an essential phrase.

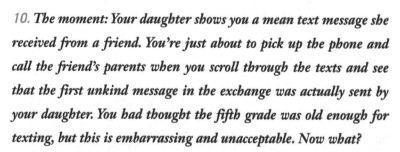

In the end, every interaction throughout your day leaves the other person a little better or a little worse. There's no such thing as a neutral exchange.

—CHICK-FIL-A FOUNDER DAN CATHY

10. The moment: Your daughter shows you a mean text message she received from a friend. You're just about to pick up the phone and call the friend's parents when you scroll through the texts and see that the first unkind message in the exchange was actually sent by your daughter. You had thought the fifth grade was old enough for texting, but this is embarrassing and unacceptable. Now what?

Pick up the phone anyway! But instead of confronting the friend's parents, simply say you're sorry for your daughter's unkind message and reassure the friend's parents that you're handling it. Then, have your daughter call (not text) the friend and issue an apology.

What's your next step? Most parents I encounter these days would tell me, "I would say, 'If that happens again, I'm taking your phone away for a week!'" As if this would send any sort of message at all.

This crucial teachable moment is best handled by taking the phone right then and there, no warnings and no threats. The same is true for whatever technology a child might use inappropriately. My daughter calls this punishment "Amish Lockdown." In my house, the way it works is that I change the passwords to all of her social media platforms, take all the apps off of her smartphone, and require her to keep her phone in the kitchen, not in her room. I've been known to replace the smartphone with an old flip phone that I keep around "just in case." ("In case" someone forgets what it means to be civil, or forgets that homework is not optional, or forgets that lying is never okay . . . you get the idea.)

Amish Lockdown works because it does many things at one time. It reminds kids that they don't need technology to live from day to day, not even to get a ride home after practice. There's this thing called planning in advance, and it works remarkably well! Eliminating or limiting technology also works because it creates time in the schedule to think about the offending action and why it is so important to avoid such behavior in the future. And most of all, it works because it reminds children that technology, and the social life it enables, are not rights but privileges that are only permitted when they're used in ways that reflect good character. Using a smartphone to send unkind, impolite messages reflects poor character, and therefore, taking it away is a natural consequence of misuse.

So that your child understands that intentional cruelty via technology and social media is a serious transgression, it's important that the teachable moment happen in real time. You might impose your penalty by saying something like, "I'm so disappointed that you abused the privilege of using a smartphone (or Facebook, or Twitter, and so on). Obviously, you need time to mature and think about how you can use these things for good, and not as a way to facilitate un-kind, un-Christian behavior. So I'm taking away the privilege of using these things until I'm convinced you're ready to try again. Keep in mind that technology is not necessary for living. I don't *have* to allow you to have access to social media or a smartphone. So in the future, if we continue to have problems with the way you use technology, I'll just cut it off entirely."

The Lesson Plan

Kids are excited when they get new technology or access to new so-cial media sites. Be sure to go over your house rules about how to use these things in positive ways, as well as the consequences for misusing them. Don't have a set of rules for tech and media? Borrow mine:

1. Technology is morally neutral; it's neither bad nor good. Use technology only for good.

2. There is NO SUCH THING as privacy in cyberspace, not even in so-called personal messages, emails, texts, di-rect messages, or SnapChats. Anything can be captured in a screenshot and sent elsewhere, or shown to someone else. Nothing you say in social media or a digital commu-nication is ever truly private.

3. Never text, email, or message anyone to complain, gossip,

hash out a disagreement, or convey your hurt feelings. Always do these things in person or in a phone call, person to person. Never use technology to avoid personal communication.

4. Do use texts, email, or messages to give compliments, praise, encouragement, send prayers, or offer support to family, friends, school mates, teammates, and so on. Be known for your kind, compassionate, and caring presence in cyberspace.

5. Never post anything on any social media platform or send any text, email, or message that you would not want to be seen by everyone you know.

6. Never use foul language in cyberspace.

7. Monitor not only your own posts but also those placed on your pages by friends and followers. You are known by the company you keep. Delete posts that are vulgar, use foul language, or make sexual or violent references. Your page should reflect your values, not your friends'.

8. Never post a compromising photo. Do not imagine that SnapChat photos or videos are really "gone" after they have been viewed. They are kept on servers and may someday be disseminated.

9. Never use technology or social media to embarrass another person.

10. Be careful that your humor is obvious and not biting.

Link to things that are appropriate and not racy. If you link to it, you "said" it.

11. Turn it off, put it down, and be present in your relationships, not virtual.

12. Misuse of technology will result in a low-tech lifestyle for as long as it takes to learn how to use this privilege responsibly.

CHAPTER FOUR

Teachable Friendship Moments

ON THE DAY I am writing this chapter, my four children have a combined total of 2,961 people as "friends," at least according to their respective Facebook pages. I'd like to think the hundreds of people each one has designated or allowed to become a "friend" reflects my children's desire to extend themselves into the larger world. I know they all have personal rules about who they'll accept as a "friend" and who they decline, and I'm relieved and proud that the guidelines they've set demonstrate a level of discernment that gives this mom comfort.

Long before "friend" became a verb associated with Facebook, we understood friendships as gifts from God to enrich our experience of his boundless love. As Christian pastor and author Charles Swindoll has so profoundly said, "I cannot even imagine where I would be today were it not for that handful of friends who have given me a heart full of joy. Let's face it; friends make life a lot more fun."

Why Kids Need Friends

Friendships are essential to a well-being of all people, and this is especially true for children and adolescents. According to Anita Gurian, PhD, and Alice Pope, PhD, writing at aboutourkids.org, the website for New York University's Child Study Center at Langone Medical Center:

> Friendships are not just a luxury; they are a necessity for healthy psychological development. Friendships are important in helping children develop emotionally and socially. They provide a training ground for trying out different ways of relating to others. Through interacting with friends, children learn the give and take of social behavior in general. They learn how to set up rules, how to weigh alternatives, and [how to] make decisions when faced with dilemmas. They experience fear, anger, aggression, and rejection. They learn how to win, how to lose, what's appropriate, what's not. They learn about social standing and power—who's in, who's out, how to lead and how to follow, what's fair and what's not. They learn that different people and different situations call for different behaviors, and they come to understand the viewpoints of other people.

Friendships offer natural teachable moments for lessons in maturity, values, and moral behavior. The subject of friendship is fertile ground for molding children's good character, helping them to rely on their consciences to make right decisions, and fostering in them the faith that serves as the foundation for the most fulfilling friendships of all.

But many of the teachable moments involving our children's friendships are just plain sticky. As much as children want and need friends in their lives, these relationships often provide uncomfortable, disappointing, and even disheartening life lessons. While family relationships rely on an assumption of shared values and beliefs, not to mention unconditional love, childhood friendships are subject to the vagaries of personality development, maturity (or immaturity!), diverse parenting and values, and a culture that seems to promote selfishness and narcissism, neither of which figures prominently in healthy relationships!

Based on my twenty-four years in the parenting trenches, as well as more than a decade of writing about children and families, I have come to this profound conclusion (grab a highlighter—you're going to want to remember this): every kid struggles. Popular kids, geeky kids, athletes, drama clubbers, band members, science whizzes, A-listers, chubby kids, skinny kids, and kids from every racial, ethnic, religious, and socioeconomic background ALL struggle. Growing up is hard! And learning by trial and error to make good friends and to be a good friend is part of the process. When we expect the struggle and convey to our children that it's normal, we can ease the pain of those grueling life lessons, but only a little tiny bit.

Friendships: Ages and Stages

There's nothing quite like the joie de vivre of preschoolers on a playground. I recall taking my children to the park when they were three and four years old, and marveling at how quickly—and authentically!—they befriended others. Kids at that age engage with and trust just about everyone (which is why we teach "stranger danger" to preschoolers). It never occurs to them that another child might not be a good friend.

By about the third grade (sometimes earlier, especially for girls), children begin to form friendships based on shared interests, personality traits, and experiences of others' behavior. Friendships in the early elementary years are still fluid as children get to know others in the neighborhood, at school, and through various activities. The expectation at this age is that most kids are friendly and guileless, the growing problem of bullying not withstanding.

There comes a point, however, when children must learn how to find and keep *good* friends. To be clear, the point is not to teach our children to judge or reject other children. Rather, it's to teach them to exhibit the qualities of a good friend and to recognize those qualities in others so that they can foster friendships that are mutual, healthy, and satisfying.

But as I said, these situations are sticky. Discernment is a lesson I have taught my kids precisely because they have experienced hurt feelings and heartache in friendships. Recall that even bad experiences don't go to waste when we're using them intentionally to mold good character, but this fact doesn't make them any easier.

Things typically get tough during the middle school years, when adolescents jockey for social prominence and power. At the same time, social media begins to define and redefine relationships in the preteen years. This potent combination frequently results in confusion and conflict as friendships evolve and sometimes dissolve.

A mistake some parents make is to work diligently to help their children "fit in" with certain social groups, rather than to help them reevaluate their social lives and look for friends with whom they share values and interests. One reason they do this is because when parents become friends with each other, it's awkward for them when their kids no longer socialize together. But strategizing with your child about how to remain or be accepted into a particular clique can send the message: "You can't be yourself and be accepted by others." Parents must reinforce the opposite lesson: "Real friends appreciate you for exactly who you are. You DO fit in—with the right group of friends!"

Discerning Good Friends

Helping children use discernment in friendship begins with a conversation about what constitutes a good friend. Suggest to your child, "Let's make a list of the attributes of a good friend. Just imagine the ideal buddy. What would he or she be like?" You'll likely hear words like "fun," "funny," "friendly," "understanding," and "nice." All good qualities for a friend, to be sure, but to build a healthy and satisfying friendship, children must learn to look deeper.

You might say, "One thing I really value is a friend that I can trust. Can you think of someone who's known for being trustworthy?" Or you could ask, "Good friends are loyal. They stick with you through thick and thin, and they're especially supportive if you're going through a hard time. Who do you know who seems like an especially loyal person?" Another trait you might describe is constancy. "Good friends don't go 'hot or cold' on you but always treat you kindly, no matter what sort of day they're having or what mood they might be in," you can explain. "Who do you know who's always kind to everyone?" By focusing on positive traits in others, you can help your child seek out the kids who are most likely to be good friends.

When kids are drawn to friendships that become negative and hurtful, you can help them evaluate those relationships using their criteria for what constitutes a good pal. You can say, "I know you enjoy a lot of things about Sam. He's funny and smart and he likes to play the same sports as you. But you have also said you value trust in a friend, and it seems each time you confide in Sam, he embarrasses you by telling others about things that were meant to be private. You may be discerning that Sam isn't as trustworthy a friend as you might like."

Discernment sometimes leads to the conclusion that certain kids simply aren't compatible or reliable friends. I trekked through this difficult discovery with each of my four children, and each one found it hard to accept that some friendships are simply not uplifting or healthy. I believe one reason that the bullying epidemic has become so problematic is that kids aren't taught to discern and choose positive friends, but instead are led to believe that they can win over friends who are consistently hurtful. Down the road in adulthood, difficult friendships can and do heal. But children must learn to set boundaries for negative relationships and spend their time seeking out good healthy friendships.

Parents can use teachable moments like the ones that follow to help guide and support children through their social struggles, and to remind them that they may not "fit" into every social group, but when they find good friends, the fit will feel just right. Situations like these will help children learn to choose good friends, and, most importantly, to be a good friend to others.

Ten Teachable Friendships Moments

> Friendship with one's self is all-important, because without it one cannot be friends with anyone else in the world.
>
> —ELEANOR ROOSEVELT

1. The moment: Your daughter has had the same compatible "bestie" since the second grade. The girls are now in middle school, and suddenly her friend seems to be "growing up" at lightning speed. She has a smartphone, uses social media, and is permitted to engage fully with pop culture. Your daughter has a traditional cell phone with limited texting. You believe she is too young for social media, and you also put limits on her media consumption. Your rules are impacting the friendship, because your daughter doesn't have access to the culture the way her bestie does. They're starting to drift apart, and your daughter feels lonely and sad.

As if parenting our children through the middle school years isn't difficult enough, what with all the hormones and confusion, these days moms and dads must also contend with the fact that entrée to media and culture have become the cornerstones on which adolescent friendships are built. A teen without Facebook, Twitter, or SnapChat, or who isn't allowed to watch MTV's Video Music Awards, may feel lost when formerly close pals gravitate to others with similar access to the culture.

Parents don't want to see their children suffer or be excluded, especially by a longtime bestie, so the temptation is to go along with what the friend is allowed to do so that your child can fit in. That's how "parenting by proxy" becomes a reality. You don't necessarily want to allow access to media—you may even believe it's harmful—but if the trade-off is a lonely daughter, you allow things that are contrary to your values. Still, a sad-faced middle schooler mustn't dictate your parenting decisions. When it comes to media and culture, it's your values, and not your children's friends, that must inform your choices.

Your policies about media create countless teachable moments, as we've already seen. As you continue to explain and demonstrate how you make decisions about media, your daughter will at least understand the rules to which she's subject. But understanding and even agreeing with your decisions doesn't make it easier to lose a bestie.

I have deep experience in the social ramifications of delaying children's participation with technology and media. We didn't allow our eldest, Kate, to use instant messaging, which meant she missed out on after-school IM chats and wasn't included when social plans were made in cyberspace. When our second daughter, Betsy, finally got a Facebook page in her senior year of high school, her friends posted on her wall, "Congratulations on becoming a regular teenager." Our son, Jimmy, was the guy whose ancient PS2 only played sports games, because we didn't allow violent video games. Suffice it to say, our house was not the place where the guys assembled to game their way through a Saturday afternoon. And our rule about cell phones (our kids got them in the summer before high school) meant our youngest daughter, Amy, was one of only a handful of eighth graders without a phone. And by "handful," I mean exactly five.

I can happily report that none of my children is worse off for his or her lack of middle school social prominence, so take heart. Your children will survive your house rules!

But delaying engagement with media isn't really the friendship issue, anyway. The heart of the matter is being excluded, and yet this can happen for any number of reasons. It's a valuable life lesson to learn to handle the hurt of exclusion, irrespective of why it occurs. So use the teachable moment of a changing friendship to teach resiliency, independence, patience, and forgiveness. You'll want to say something like, "I can only imagine how hard it is to see your best friend get closer to other kids when you two have been close for so long. But friendships go through different seasons, and I imagine you'll get closer again when the novelty of her ability to use media wears off a bit. And when you get a little older, you'll also have more access to social media and pop culture. In the meantime, there are probably other kids you can get to know better who might also have similar rules about media. When you have that in common, it can make it easier."

Invariably, your daughter will tell you she is the only person in your ZIP code without access to media. According to the Pew Research Center's report "Teens and Technology 2013," 78 percent of teens (ages twelve to seventeen) have cell phones, and almost half of them have smartphones (47 percent). About three quarters of teens surveyed reported that they access the Internet at least occasionally on a mobile device. That feels like "everybody" when you're twelve.

That's when you remind your child that your decisions are always in her best interest, even if they seem hard to accept, and that finding other friends will be easy . . . because they'll be the kids who aren't looking down at a smartphone.

> **Watch out for the joy-stealers:**
> **gossip, criticism, complaining, faultfinding,**
> **and a negative, judgmental attitude.**
> —JOYCE MEYER

2. The moment: Your daughter comes home from soccer practice, having been driven in a carpool by the mother of a friend on her team, and lets you know that during the ride home, the mother, her daughter, and another friend gossiped about a teammate. Your daughter reports that she sat quietly and uncomfortably, but felt pressured to agree with the unkind things that were said. She feels guilty for nodding and laughing along. Should you confront the mother? And what's the lesson for your daughter?

Sadly, one of the issues in today's character crisis is that too many adults don't behave in an exemplary fashion. Instead, they're modeling behaviors that reflect poor character, or, at the least, bad judgment. You'd hope that a mother would admonish the girls in her carpool, "Now, now, ladies. If you can't say something nice, don't say anything at all." Instead, it's not uncommon for moms to jump into the fray of gossip and condemnation.

I'm not a fan of confronting adults in such situations unless relationships and circumstances warrant a one-on-one conversation, and then only if the chat can be friendly and constructive. Besides, the purpose of this book is to help you understand how to use unfortunate circumstances like this one to teach lessons to your children about character and conscience.

A talk with your daughter might go something like this: "It's unfortunate that the conversation in the carpool took place, and I'm disappointed that Mrs. Smith participated in it and didn't stop the girls from gossiping. It's disturbing that a parent would do such a thing, but adults make mistakes, too. The crucial thing is that you learn from this experience."

You can appreciate the difficult spot your daughter was in but still hold her accountable for her actions by saying, "I can imagine it felt uncomfortable to be caught off guard when the group in the car started talking about another girl, but it's so important to learn from this mistake. Gossip is always destructive, and participating in it, even by nodding along or laughing, hurts everyone involved. Respecting others doesn't mean we will always agree with someone or even that we like to spend time with that person, but it does mean we don't say hurtful things behind another person's back."

Your daughter knows her participation was wrong, which shows that her conscience is functioning, and it's bothering her. This is good! Feeling guilty is how we know we've made mistakes. Rather than assuage her guilt, help her to understand her responsibility in such a situation by saying, "You may not be able to control the situation or make other people stop gossiping, but you can make it clear by your reaction that the conversation makes you uncomfortable. That's what it means to have the courage of your convictions. When you know something is wrong, you have to act accordingly."

Not only can you use an episode like this to reinforce your lessons about character, you can also strategize about what your child could do differently when faced with a similar situation. Behaving as if she's visibly uncomfortable is a start, but she might also speak up and say, "I'd rather not talk about a teammate behind her back. It makes me feel bad." You can even role-play so your daughter can practice her response. Eventually, she'll become a person who is known for her opposition to gossip and her unwillingness to tolerate it.

Finally, unkind episodes like this can be used to remind kids to pray for forgiveness when they make mistakes, and also to pray for each other. Considering gossip in the context of your Christian faith allows you to call it what it is—a sin—and helps you connect good character with the desire to obey God. When children realize that their peers are targets of cruelty, their faith calls them to reach out, support others, and extend Christ's love in everyday situations. That's the best response of all.

> **Even as kids reach adolescence, they need more than ever for us to watch over them. Adolescence is not about letting go. It's about hanging on during a very bumpy ride.**
> —RON TAFFEL

3. The moment: Your eighth grade son tells you over dinner that in a conversation at the school lunch table, "All the guys say that drinking, smoking weed, and hooking up with girls are just normal things during high school. They all say their parents have told them about the crazy things they did back in their high school years, and they know we'll do that stuff too." According to your son, other parents are only concerned that their kids act "responsibly"—for example, using condoms, or not drinking and driving—actions that might limit the risks of experimental behavior. How can you influence your teen when the perception is that experimentation is the norm?

To be sure, disconcerting percentages of teens drink, use drugs, and become sexually active during high school, and the physical, emotional, and spiritual risks associated with these choices are serious. According to the 2011 Youth Risk Behavior Survey from the US Department of Health and Human Services (HHS), 39 percent of teens had consumed alcohol; 22 percent had engaged in binge drinking, 8 percent drove after drinking, and 24 percent rode in a car with a driver who'd been drinking (all within the thirty days prior to the survey). HHS also reports that about a third of high school seniors say they have used marijuana (within in the year before the survey) and that sexual activity is high among high schoolers. The HHS Youth Risk survey found 47 percent reporting they have had intercourse; 15 percent say they have had sex with three or more different partners.

And it's no wonder that eighth graders already anticipate the risky behaviors they'll undertake in high school: many engage in those activities while still in middle school. For example, a study from the University of Michigan's Monitoring the Future research program concludes that fully a third of eighth graders have tried drinking, including 13 percent who reported drinking within the month before the survey.

But despite what these statistics suggest, risky conduct isn't really a "new norm." Plenty of kids make it all the way through high school without engaging in dangerous experimental behaviors. In my parenting journey, I learned it might all come down to one simple yet profound realization: Children tend to meet us where we expect to find them.

When parents expect that teens will drink, use drugs, or have sex during their teen years, their children recognize that these behaviors will be considered normal, even if they know their parents don't approve of them. On the other hand, parents can have a powerful influence when they communicate to their adolescent and teenage kids, "I expect that you're capable of using self-control and good judgment, and that you won't make dangerous choices about drinking, drugs, and sex."

Stating our expectations for our children came instinctively to my husband and me. In fact, when our older kids started to go out with friends during high school, I got in the habit of saying goodbye with a warm but explicit reminder about what I expected. "No drinking, no drugs, no sex, and have fun!" They'd roll their eyes as they left to get ice cream or go to a football game, but the point was clear: I never pretended that such activities couldn't happen, so I wanted our parental pressure to be greater than the peer pressure they might encounter in their social spheres.

It turns out my gut instinct was dead-on: If you stay close to your kids, and if you're crystal clear about your expectations for their behavior, the chances drop significantly that they'll engage in risky activities. According to the Partnership for a Drug-Free America (drugfree.org), "Research shows that when parents talk openly about drugs and drinking, children have better self-control and develop more negative perceptions of these risky behaviors." And a study published in the *Journal of the American Board of Family Medicine* concludes, "Parental direction has a powerful effect on the reduction of risk behavior in young adolescents. A limited ability for abstract reasoning during early adolescence requires clear anticipatory guidance by parents and an active effort to maintain communication in the child-parent relationship."

Even more importantly, a 2011 story from *ScienceDaily* (Science Daily.com) reveals research that proves parents can influence their children's behavior even after they head off to college. Specifically, the report cites a study published in the *Journal of Youth and Adolescence* by researchers from Brigham Young University in which students who said they were close to their fathers were less likely to use drugs or engage in sex, while those who said they were close to their moms were less likely to drink alcohol. "The protective effect of mothers' awareness was more pronounced when the students also felt close to their mom. Under those circumstances, the researchers found that students were less likely to be involved in any of the three risk behavior categories studied: drugs, alcohol and risky sexual activity." (Go moms!)

Which brings us back to the dinner table and our teachable moment. For the sake of this discussion, I imagined a scenario in which a son mentions a conversation with his peers that troubles him. That sort of thing does happen, but not as often as we'd hope. More likely, you'll have to tease this kind of conversation out by asking leading questions and creating an atmosphere in which your adolescent child feels he can speak frankly.

When he does, you can say, "Wow. It's kind of scary that the guys are already anticipating making bad decisions, isn't it? And it's disturbing to us, as parents, that some adults almost enable their kids to make poor choices, or at least send the signal that it's expected. It worries us that some of your friends' parents aren't taking as strong a stand as we are about what to expect in high school."

It's crucial to then say: "We love you and we want you to make smart decisions in high school, but just as importantly, we have confidence in you. You're a great kid and we know you want to be successful and safe, and that you want to have fun in high school, and you can do all of those things without using drugs or alcohol and without becoming sexually active. There may be times when it's difficult to walk the straight and narrow path, but we're going to be there to support you and make it as easy as possible to do the right things."

I wouldn't assess the character of the guys at the lunch table, other than to observe that high school is a time when lots of good kids make poor decisions. I would, however, remind my son that high school will be a time when he can meet many new kids, and that he should use his skills of discernment to find friends who like to have fun without engaging in high-risk behaviors.

> **I wish we could all get along like we used to in middle school. I wish I could bake a cake filled with rainbows and smiles and everyone would eat and be happy.**
>
> —THE CRYING GIRL, *MEAN GIRLS*

4. The moment: Your daughter calls a friend to see if she's available to come over on a Friday evening. The friend's mom answers and says, "Oh, she already left for the sleepover, honey," assuming your daughter was also invited to a gathering of their friends. When your daughter hangs up, she realizes that a "secret" several of her friends were discussing during the week must have been about the sleepover, to which she was not invited. Your daughter is devastated, and you're just plain angry. What lesson do you teach in this hurtful moment?

Some situations inherently teach universal life lessons: People can be unkind. Friendships are fickle. Growing up is hard. Life isn't fair. When my kids learned they were excluded from social functions, their reactions reflected incredulity: "Why wouldn't someone want to invite *me*?" It's impossible not to take such a circumstance personally. Inevitably, kids go searching for an explanation and end up feeling insecure.

You might be tempted to pick up the phone and call the host mom to find out why your daughter was left off the invitation list. Resist this urge! I tried it a couple of times, and can attest that this is not a strategy that will help your child or improve her situation. It's possible this course of action is how I came to appreciate the wisdom in that adage about preparing "the child for the path."

After some deep, cleansing breaths ("breathe in grace, breathe out peace"), focus on how you can use these crummy, hurtful, and unnecessary bumps on the road to build up your child's character and help her to become stronger and more resilient. These traits will serve her in the present circumstance and in the future, too.

How you specifically handle such a teachable moment depends in part on the age of your child. Surprisingly, younger children up to about age ten can be somewhat philosophical. You can suggest that parents sometimes set limits on the number of guests that can be invited to a sleepover, and you can also remind your child of times when she was included in social events and other kids were not. (An empathy lesson—bonus points!) Parents can usually talk a nine-year-old into believing that she'll be invited to the next sleepover, and it certainly helps to divert her attention by baking cookies or having an impromptu movie night at home. The point is, younger children needn't indulge their feelings for too long, as childhood friendships are fluid. Things change quickly and will probably improve soon.

But just wait. That sweet girl of yours will turn twelve and quickly understand that cliques are real, and the structure of those social circles can have a pivotal impact on her friendships and social opportunities. Girl World is a stressful and often hurtful place to grow up, and most adolescent girls experience at least some of the fallout of being on the wrong side of the "Popular Girls," even if it's just learning to steer clear of them.

I want to emphasize that some aspects of adolescent female behavior have been rightly redefined as bullying, rather than social aggression, and that this book is not meant as a resource for victims of bullying, per se. Bullying is serious and dangerous, and there are excellent resources for parents on combating and responding to bullying (see this chapter's endnotes at the end of this book for helpful resources). If you think your child is being victimized, don't wait for it to blow over. Become a strong and vocal advocate for his or her safety and well-being.

Girls can experience insidious behavior that undercuts their self-esteem and self-confidence. A girl knows it when she sees it: Conversations that stop when she approaches a group of friends, or that are full of inside jokes and references she doesn't get. Backs that turn at the lunch table—not enough to exclude her entirely, but just enough to make it hard for her to hear a conversation. Being the last one selected when work groups form for class projects. These encounters can't be called overtly cruel, but they're enough to make sure a girl knows she's not in the inner circle.

To understand how Girl World works, author and adolescent expert Rosalind Wiseman's seminal *New York Times* bestseller *Queen Bees and Wannabes: Helping Your Daughter Survive Cliques, Gossip, Boyfriends, and Other Realities of Adolescence* is a must-read for parents of daughters. Comedian Tina Fey turned Wiseman's research-based book into the hit 2004 film *Mean Girls*, a hilarious movie precisely because it's so uncomfortably true. My daughters know every word of the script, because for girls, it's shorthand.

Hard as these hurtful experiences are to process (and the one I used above as "the moment" is not hypothetical; it really happened to one of my daughters), they can create some of the most tender and transformative life lessons. Assuming the treatment your daughter encounters falls short of bullying, her life will present opportunities for teachable moments about resilience, staying positive in difficult circumstances, being brave, and discerning good friends from bad.

My first reaction in these moments was always to hug and listen. Granted, it's hard to understand what a preteen is saying through the blubbering and nose-blowing, but allowing the expression of raw emotion is important. At the moment when your child realizes she has been excluded—or worse, betrayed—by her friends, your unconditional love and support are essential.

When the tears subside, ask some leading questions that will help your daughter understand if she's missing social cues. As much as we'd like to think our children are always socially adept, they sometimes make missteps that can be the cause of their social dilemmas. You might say, "Tell me about the way you interact with the other girls. Do you feel like they listen to you when you talk? Do they seem to treat you the same way they treat each other?" Perhaps she's trying too hard to hang with a group that will never be accepting, and while it's tempting to judge the kids who exclude your child, your role is to help her find friends who appreciate and value her, not get angry about the ones who don't. A conversation with her about the attributes of a good friend, and a joint assessment of whether the friends she is pursuing reflect her criteria, can help her draw the conclusion that she may need to look for a more accepting social group.

It's also possible that your daughter did something you don't know about that caused her to be excluded. Kids aren't quick to run home and tell you their transgressions, but all children mess up from time to time. An episode like this one is a good time to take stock of how your daughter is behaving with her peers. If you discover there's a conflict you weren't aware of, your teachable moment should focus on seeking forgiveness, making amends, and helping your daughter to recognize that she can improve her situation by taking responsibility.

Finally, whenever my kids found themselves on the outside looking in, I made it a point to remind them that they can never feel left out at home. We humans are pack animals, but kids must learn that the first pack is the family, despite the nearly constant cultural drumbeat that it's all about their peers. Though it's always painful to see our kids get hurt, I cherished those times when coming to their emotional rescue created precious moments of TLC at home.

When I was labeled stupid, that scarred me forever.
—TERRY BRADSHAW

5. The moment: As you are driving away from the school pickup line, your kids point to a fifth-grade boy, a classmate of your son's, who is standing on the walkway waiting for his ride. They announce, "Everyone knows he's gay," a conclusion based on the fact that he's not particularly athletic, likes being in plays and the school choir, dresses in "hipster" styles, usually hangs out with a group of girls, and generally seems different from other guys. What lessons should you focus on in this teachable moment?

One reason I strenuously object to the overreach of the gay agenda into American childhood is that kids aren't mature enough to understand or appreciate the significance of their casual declarations about the possible sexuality of their peers. Since I'm not a sociologist, I can't prove my conclusion, but common sense tells me that the more we "inform and educate" kids about same-sex attraction and Lesbian, Gay, Bi-Sexual, Transgender, Queer/Questioning (LGBTQ) issues during their early, formative years, the more problems we create for children who are not gay but simply different.

The media and the public educational system now force parents to teach young children about homosexuality and same-sex attraction at ages when youngsters absolutely should not be contemplating such topics. Adding complexity to an already-confusing subject, Christian parents must teach our children the truth about the sin of homosexual behavior while making the distinction that we are not to judge others.

Once children are informed about what it means to "be gay," human nature kicks in, and they try to figure out who among their peers falls under this label. Who could be easier to label "gay" than an artsy fifth-grade boy? Or an athletic girl who once would have been merely known as a "tomboy"? Children who are simply going about the business of growing and maturing, exploring their interests and exuding their natural personalities, now are burdened by culturally suggested labels.

The flip side of the issue of labeling is the inclination, based on cultural pressure, to accept and celebrate homosexuality as proof that we accept and love others. The pro-gay agenda now aggressively promotes the idea that children should "come out" as gay or transgendered even in early elementary school, a time when many, if not most, kids are confused about issues of sex and sexuality. Such a premature declaration cannot possibly reflect a mature understanding of one's sexual self, yet organizations such as the Gay-Straight Alliance Network believe children should be supported in self-identifying as gay or transgendered and be celebrated for doing so.

Christian parents face big challenges on this subject, so any mention that a schoolmate might be gay introduces an important teachable moment. Your first goal is to halt any future conversations that label another child by saying, "It is never okay to casually call a boy 'gay' or to speculate about whether a girl is a lesbian. Kids act in all sorts of normal ways that have nothing to do with their sexuality, and it is unfair and unkind to label people based on their personalities or interests. Whether a child turns out to be homosexual is none of our concern, but what is our concern is to protect the dignity and reputation of everyone in our school community. Kids should be able to be who they are without focusing on their sexuality, and it's wrong for you to speculate about it."

Of course, the culture being what it is, there's a strong likelihood a friend or acquaintance of your child will divulge that he or she is gay. What's the takeaway when this happens? Similarly, it's to keep the focus off the issue of sexuality, no matter how intent the friend may be on bringing it to the forefront. Counsel your kids to be kind and respectful, but to draw boundaries around these conversations. They can learn to say, "We're friends and I respect you, but I'm not comfortable talking about sexuality. It's just not a subject I want to discuss, okay?"

As I revealed in my book *Don't Let the Kids Drink the Kool-Aid: Confronting the Assault on Our Families, Faith, and Future*, the success of the gay agenda hinges on normalizing homosexual behavior for our children's generation, and even introducing the idea of "sexual fluidity"—the idea that a person's biological gender is not what determines sexual identity or sexual preference. Proponents of these ideas are so entrenched in pop culture and in our public schools that the issue of gay or transgendered friends is absolutely going to be one that most parents will have to confront at one time or another.

I'm aware that I can be annoying.
—SANDRA BULLOCK

6. The moment: Your son has a large and friendly group of buddies, but one of the boys in the group is . . . quirky. Your son finds him downright

"annoying" and demonstrates a lack of patience with the boy, which bothers you. But seeing them interact, you can also understand why your son struggles with this friend. He lacks social skills and he's often at the center of misunderstandings. When your son complains about "the annoying kid," what can you teach that will mold his character?

Perhaps the first lesson that kids need to know is that the "quirky" kids often turn out to be the Bill Gateses of the world!

While we might wish that all children could get along easily, some kids just don't click, for whatever reason. Children's personalities, while still growing and developing, are unique and can sometimes grate on each other. So one lesson is that it's okay not to like everyone equally well. Kids should have permission to like whom they like, and to sometimes be annoyed by a peer.

Being annoyed and being rude are two different things, however. In a teachable moment about an annoying friend, you could say, "I know you and this kid just don't click, but you have friends in common, and you are obligated to treat him kindly even though his personality grates on you a little bit. Learning to be patient with people you find annoying is something you'll need to do throughout your life. We don't get to just dismiss some folks because their personalities don't mesh easily with ours. And you never know—he may find you annoying, too! The trick is to be patient and friendly, and if you find yourself running short of patience, keep some distance. It's not okay to hurt someone's feelings just because his personality doesn't match yours."

Often, when kids use self-discipline to be patient with an "annoying kid," they unwittingly get to know that child better, and, almost without noticing, they discover that the "annoying kid" has become a close pal. The key to getting to this point is the exercise of good manners, being polite and kind to everyone out of respect for their dignity.

When making social plans or hosting birthday parties, is it okay to exclude a peer your child finds annoying? Yes and no. If he's having just a few kids over to play, you needn't require that your child invite everyone in his social group. But if it's a large gathering, such as a birthday party, there's a great life lesson in including even the kid your child finds challenging. You could remind him, "Leaving one friend off the list will make it awkward for everyone else, and besides, a birthday party should be a celebration of friendship, not a reason to make someone feel left out."

Humans are made as sexual beings; thus, sexuality is a gift that must be stewarded.
—YOUTH MINISTER JUSTIN SPURLOCK

7. The moment: Your high school daughter tells you that a friend of hers has confided that she and her boyfriend are thinking of taking their relationship to the "next level," meaning they're planning to become sexually active. Your daughter is deeply troubled that her friend is making a mistake and wants your advice about what to say. How can you help your daughter to give good counsel and also use this as a teachable moment about premarital sex?

These types of situations are difficult for parents who care not only about their own children but about the well-being of their kids' friends as well. Often, a sense of responsibility tugs at us to get in-volved as a parental figure for other children. But should you insert yourself in the above situation? It depends on a host of variables, in-cluding how well you know the friend and her family, and the nature of your daughter's relationship with this friend. Sometimes teens are more receptive to the advice and counsel of adults other than their parents, so an opportunity to offer good advice shouldn't be passed over.

If the relationship and circumstances seem fitting, you might try to engineer a heart-to-heart conversation with both girls, in which you could say, "I know you're thinking about becoming more inti-mate with your boyfriend, and I just want to be sure you're really thinking through all of the ramifications of that decision." In that sort of conversation, your primary goal should be to convince the friend to talk to her parents before she takes that next step.

But let's assume you're not able to have a direct conversation with your daughter's friend. This situation allows you to help your daughter understand the gravity of the decision to become sexually active and to be able to articulate those factors to her friend. Given the high percentage of sexually active teens, you want to be sure she knows where you stand on this issue, and that she has thought it through for herself. Besides, this won't be the last time your daugh-ter will be asked for advice, so it's a teachable moment for her to learn to prepare for serious conversations in which she's counted on to give her best counsel to a friend.

Situations such as this ought to begin with an open-ended ques-tion to get your child talking. You could say, "Wow . . . this is serious. How do you feel about it, and what do you think?" You may discover that your daughter has thought it through and is ready to give excellent advice; she just needs your support to articulate her opinions and speak courageously.

You might encourage her by saying, "It's a big responsibility to be asked for advice, especially on such a serious and potentially life-changing subject, but God has put you in a position to offer wisdom and guidance. So the first thing to recognize is that the Holy Spirit is the one who's really going to be giving your friend advice. All you have to do is approach this topic both lovingly and candidly."

Encourage your daughter to be brave when she counsels her friend. "You need to say, 'I care about you so much so I have to be completely truthful. I think you'll be making a big mistake if you decide to be sexually active. You may think you're in love—and you might even end up together, because some people do marry their high school sweethearts. But if you really love each other, you won't risk all the things that could happen to your futures by sleeping together. There's no such thing as "safe sex." There's always the risk that you could get pregnant or contract a sexually transmitted disease. But more than that, sex elevates a relationship in a way that no other expression can do. If you're not really mature enough for the emotional bonds that go with it, you can be deeply hurt. So you should never take that next step unless you're also ready and willing to handle all the ramifications of that decision.'"

Such encounters allow our children to be witnesses for Christ in a powerful way. You can remind your daughter of this by saying, "Whenever you get the chance to be a witness to a friend, as in this situation, you should always speak the truth in love. You could say, 'I believe God's plan for sex is to build up marriages; I don't believe it's meant for high schoolers who are going out and want to feel closer.' "

When our teens find themselves in the position of counselor to a friend, they should always encourage their friends to talk to their parents or other trusted adults. You can suggest that they introduce their friends to a pastor or youth minister. As they get older, they can become equipped to encourage and inspire their friends toward smart and mature (and godly!) choices. Teaching kids to be strong peer counselors just happens to strengthen their understanding of crucial life lessons, as well, so it's a teachable moment that keeps teaching over and over.

> **You can only be young once.**
> **But you can always be immature.**
> —DAVE BARRY

8. The moment: Your fourth grade daughter comes home from school in distress. Her friends repeatedly accuse her of cheating while playing a game on the playground at lunch. She insists she doesn't cheat, but the group won't believe her. The issue has gone on for weeks and won't die out. What can you teach your daughter about fairness and justice?

It is convenient that I have four children who offer such a plethora of material for a parenting book! This is not a hypothetical scenario. It happened to Betsy. The game was Blind Man's Bluff, and for reasons she still doesn't understand (did I mention she's a college grad?), her posse of pals decided she always peeked. She claims she was just good at the game. It's still a sore subject, poor thing.

What I taught her in that moment was that sometimes we're just misjudged, plain and simple. You can be as right as rain, but sometimes people will believe what they decide is the truth, and nothing you can say or do will convince them otherwise. I think I said something like, "Betsy, the good news is that in the fourth grade, things like this blow over quickly. Take a book outside on the playground, find a comfy spot on a bench or under a tree, and take a break from Blind Man's Bluff. Pretty soon your friends will get bored with the game, or realize you made it more fun, and everything will be fine." And it was.

Sometimes the lessons we teach in those moments aren't heavy or ethical or deeply philosophical; they're just the common-sense coping skills that help people manage and maintain relationships. "Take a break from the drama, find some shade, and read a book" is a lifesaver that works well into adulthood!

> **It is one of the blessings of old friends**
> **that you can afford to be stupid with them.**
> —RALPH WALDO EMERSON

9. The moment: Your seventh grade son comes home in tears of frustration and anger after spending the afternoon down the street at his buddy's house. He and this friend get along wonderfully when it's just the two of them, but when other guys are included, as was the case this day, your son is the easy target who is teased and picked on. You learn that the afternoon included several conflicts in which your son kept telling the guys to stop teasing, but the more he protested, the worse it got. Your son finally left in a huff when none of the

guys would take seriously the game of Monopoly they were playing.
Where to begin in this teachable moment?

I'll never forget the sound of the slamming back door when my son stomped into the house on the day this episode took place. He slumped down in a chair in the living room, clenched his fists on his knees, and said something like, "Grrrrrrr!" I had to pretend I didn't think he was adorable. (I rallied! I'm not that insensitive!)

The truth is, my kids were fairly geeky in middle school, and geeky kids are easy targets. My son, Jimmy, withstood his fair share of needling from the guys, but his best friend was always fun and friendly unless some of the cooler guys were around. Then, playing to his audience, no doubt, he joined in the teasing and made Jimmy feel like the odd guy out.

On the particular summer night that this teachable moment presented itself, I had help from my two older daughters, who shared their wisdom about middle school social survival. What ensued was a hilarious evening of storytelling as each daughter tried to outdo the other with tales of social anxiety, awkward moments, and friendship foibles. The lesson, of course, was that everybody struggles, and that Jimmy would get through his frequent bouts of frustration if he could laugh at himself a little more readily and disarm the cool kids with an easygoing nature.

We had perked Jimmy up, but the real teachable moment happened when the phone rang. It was his friend, calling to apologize for teasing Jimmy all day, and we heard Jimmy say, "I'm sorry too, for being such a hothead. I should have just laughed it off." They joked a little more and the next day, all was right with the world.

If only teachable moments were always that much fun!

> There's no tragedy in life
> like the death of a child. Things never
> get back to the way they were.
> —DWIGHT D. EISENHOWER

10. The moment: A boy at your child's high school commits suicide. He was a popular and accomplished student, the kind of boy no one would ever expect to take his own life, and your children are devastated and confused. How can you parent them through this tragedy and help them learn from it?

I wish with all my heart that I didn't have the experience to address this question with authority, but several years ago, Jim and I supported dear friends through the death of their son following a long battle with depression, ending in his suicide. In addition, two students from our children's high school have taken their lives in the years since our kids have been enrolled there. The death of a young person is always tragic, but death by suicide is uniquely confusing and heartbreaking.

In our advanced society, where common childhood diseases have been all but eradicated, the death of a minor is likely to be sudden and distressing. According to the Centers for Disease Control and Prevention, the five most common causes of death for teenagers aged twelve to nineteen are accidents or unintentional injuries, homicide, suicide, cancer, and heart disease. More specifically, the American Academy of Child and Adolescent Psychiatry reports that suicide is the third leading cause of death for fifteen- to twenty-four-year-olds, and the sixth leading cause of death for five- to fourteen-year-olds.

While the death of a young person is always tragic, there's nothing so heart-wrenching as the suicide of a peer, because it creates questions and fears—especially among teenagers, who are naturally vulnerable and emotional. Even if they didn't know the person well, kids are left to wonder whether they could have done or said something that might have "caused" the person to give up on life, or whether they could have done something to prevent it. Guilt and confusion are even greater for kids who lose a good friend to suicide. They can't help but assume that they could or should have done something different to prevent their friend from killing himself.

Whether or not your child is closely acquainted with a victim of suicide, you should respond to such a death in your school or community by talking openly and candidly about it with him or her. Typically, schools provide parents with resources to help you address your child's potential concerns—use those. Mental health professionals have gleaned good insight into the minds and responses of teenagers to peer suicide. As a parent, you're smart to avail yourself of that wisdom.

My experiences in the aftermath of teen suicides have taught me that the thing my children wanted most was reassurance. They wanted to be told that their own struggles were normal and wouldn't lead them to self-destructive behaviors. They wanted to know that they were strong enough to endure the stresses in their lives; they wanted to be certain that Jim and I were watching over them and keeping them safe. Seeing the grief and turmoil of the families left behind, my children have reacted by clinging a little more closely to me, reaching frequently for hugs and the strength and confidence they communicate.

Sharing the walk with friends through the suicide of their son was nothing short of brutal, but it also proved to be a unique experience of faith, and a tangible way to prove that God is real, and present, and loving. Despite being devastated by our friends' loss, we were able to demonstrate to our children that our faith in Jesus Christ allowed us to be hopeful, and even to be joyful, in the midst of trauma. In the teachable moments of a dark and distressing January night, we held each of our kids close and told them over and over that we loved them, and that God loves them, and that we would always be there for them. That's about all you can do, but it is enough.

When confronted with the news of the death of a teenager, you must deal with the cruel reality of death, but you can also focus on life. Our children deserve the comfort and assurance that life prevails. Life sustains. Life wins. Life is God's promise to us, because Christ conquered death and earned our redemption for us.

In a culture that seems to glorify death but is then shocked when evil snatches the innocent from our midst, we must teach our children that life is precious, and precarious, and sweet . . . and eternal.

The Lesson Plan

Staying focused on the real task at hand—molding our children's character—is the only way we will help them learn to navigate their friendship journeys while also standing for their values and convictions. In those times when our kids struggle in friendships, it's hard not to step in and resolve the issues, or come to our children's defense. Among the many ways in which parenting is meant to humble us, though, is the fact that our children are just as likely as their friends to be at fault when conflicts arise.

Here are a few basic principles to keep in mind as you raise up a great friend:

- *Everybody struggles,* so don't be surprised or incredulous when your children have friendship issues. They come with the territory as kids grow and mature.

- *Help children find friends who support and reflect their values.* When friends share common values as well as common interests, the foundation of friendship is solid.

- *When friendship issues arise, don't only solve the immediate problem; look for the larger life lesson.* Use those snags in the road to teach lessons that promote good character and develop a strong moral compass.

- *Live by the adage "Prepare the child for the path, not the path for the child."* You can't always make things socially smooth for children, so your first priority is to instill character, conscience, and faith. These are the things that will allow your children to foster and maintain great friendships throughout their lives.

CHAPTER FIVE

Teachable Moments at School

AND NOW, FOR SOME math: by the time my four children complete the twelfth grade, they will have spent a combined 9,360 days in elementary and secondary schools, give or take. My kids were never fans of school lunches, so I tend to think of that number in terms of turkey sandwiches, juice pouches, and Oreos. We all have our devices to mark time. My device is the brown paper lunch sack.

My husband, Jim, and I chose to take advantage of the Catholic elementary school associated with our parish, and then sent our children to the only Catholic high school in our community. Being Catholic Christians, we wanted to provide an educational environment that would help us instill the faith and values we hold dear, and we wanted our kids to be immersed in their Catholic identity so that they could be light and salt to the larger world.

Jim and I are both products of public schools. He attended K-12; I went to Catholic elementary schools and then a public high school. We hold public educators in high esteem. Still, though we live in an excellent school district, we opted for a Christian education for our children beyond our belief in the particular mission of Catholic schools. Namely, there is undeniable evidence that public schools are being used to advance social and political agendas that conflict with our moral and religious beliefs. (At the risk of shameless self-promotion, and because it's too much information to include here, I refer you again to my previous book, *Don't Let the Kids Drink the Kool-Aid*, in which I document the cultural and political influences on American education, especially on teacher preparation and curriculum development.)

This is not to say that all teachers engage in social engineering. Across America, and right there in your child's school, there are excellent teachers and administrators who are dedicated to providing children with a solid educational foundation. But even teachers admit they are now subject to an overarching agenda of secular progressivism that has forced its way into their classrooms, dictating lessons and values in direct opposition to the Christian doctrine espoused by the vast majority of Americans.

Rest assured this secular—some would say radical—agenda will present you with countless teachable moments as your children matriculate.

The Purpose of Public Schools

As long as we're examining the ways in which the culture impacts our children's school experiences, let's consider the original purpose of

America's system of public education. The first compulsory education laws were adopted in Massachusetts, the most famous of which
was the Commonwealth's 1647 statute known as the "Old Deluder
Satan Law." Its purpose was to enable people to read the Bible, and
thus avoid sin. The first *New-England Primer* is said to have taught
the alphabet using Bible verses that began with each letter. I can't get
a copy of the version from 1690, so I'm going to trust the Internet
on that fact.

The historical mission of our nation's schools is perhaps best de-
lineated in the Northwest Ordinance of 1787, adopted by the Continental Congress to govern the emerging western territories, in
which Section 14, Article 4 states, "Religion, morality, and knowledge, being necessary to good government and the happiness of
mankind, schools and the means of education shall forever be encouraged."

Schools operated under this general mission, reflecting the
Judeo-Christian foundations of our nation's formation, until the
early 1960s, when the combined impact of three United States
Supreme Court decisions eliminated from the public schools any
school-sponsored prayer, individual prayer, and the recitation
of sacred scripture for the purpose of prayer. Individual, voluntary,
student-led prayer ultimately remained a constitutional right, and
the Bible and other religious works may be used as literary texts.

Anecdotally, "taking God out of the public schools" is often cited
as the reason for problems in our educational system and society in
general. (Surely you've received that email that's been floating
around since the dawn of the Internet?) But I believe the oft-cited
"separation of church and state" within our schools is just one slice

of a big, multilayered cultural-social-political pie. It's bigger than prayer in schools. It's bigger than sex ed. It's bigger than multiculturalism and diversity.

It's the all-encompassing idea that public schools are meant to serve as institutions for social change and the doing of "social justice." When schools are used for these purposes, the rights, expectations, and wishes of parents to direct the education and instruction of their children take a back seat to the indoctrination that is accomplished through the school environment, policies, and curriculum.

What's on the Agenda?

In addition to situations that typically arise in the school setting, four main topics challenge the values and beliefs taught in Christian homes:

Comprehensive sexuality education, which is being adopted widely across the nation, is based on the assumption that adolescents will naturally and appropriately become sexually active during their teen years. These programs also promote progressive ideas about sexuality, such as the normalization of homosexuality and the idea that gender identity is determined not by physiology but by the feelings of the individual. Comprehensive programs begin in the earliest school years (yup, kindergarten) with so-called "age appropriate" lessons about sexual development, emotional attachment, attraction, and gender identity.

The normalization of homosexuality included in the curriculum for comprehensive sexuality education is also promoted through school safety programs to prevent bullying. Importantly, though, while states still permit parents to opt their children out of sex education classes, they do not allow students to be excused from programs that promote school safety. The designation of homosexuals as a minority group has also prompted one state, California, to mandate that the "contributions of gays" must be included in all subjects, in the same manner that women and other minorities are singled out and recognized. California is a leading purchaser of textbooks, so that state's law will influence what is taught across the nation in the years to come.

Religious liberty and freedom of expression in the public square, and particularly in public schools, remain under attack, especially Christian expression. While secular student groups are among the fastest growing clubs in America's public schools, Christian and other religious students often find themselves targeted under the faux doctrine of "separation of church and state," which appears nowhere in our Constitution.

The elimination of American patriotism as a cultural value in favor of multiculturalism and diversity also is a dominant idea that now dictates curriculum and programming in public schools. In addition, political correctness in the classroom is robbing children of the opportunity to grow up naturally and playfully, and instead is instilling in them self-consciousness and over-sensitivity.

In short, Christian parents whose children attend public schools now are inherently at odds with some of the primary goals of American public education, and that means you're going to be faced with many teachable moments that require you to differentiate between the values taught at school and the beliefs you are teaching in your home. Even if you send your children to private or religious schools, they may use state-mandated curriculum and textbooks, and certified teachers all attend the same schools of education, where some of the most radical members of academe are ensconced. So choosing a private or religious school won't eliminate all of the issues that concern parents.

The ways in which these cultural and political points of view exhibit themselves in America's schools is almost surreal. Here are just a few examples from the past few years:

- A group in Brookline, Massachusetts, worked to ban the Pledge of Allegiance from its school district on the grounds that reciting it is "un-American" and also might promote bullying of students who refuse to say it.

- A student in Fort Worth, Texas, was suspended for expressing privately to another student, unrelated to the content of the German class in which they were talking, that his Christian beliefs taught him that homosexuality is wrong. The teacher, overhearing the private comment, sent the student to the principal's office for disciplinary action—not for holding a side conversation during class, but for opposing homosexuality.

- A mother in the Sierra Sands Unified School District in California learned from her kindergarten and third grade daughters that a male employee of the school cafeteria came to work attired in make-up and a tank top, revealing a bra with exposed straps. The district claimed "its hands were tied" because, while the attire in question would not be permitted for students, it could not limit a transvestite from dressing in drag for work, even if such behavior disrupts the learning environment.

• Before the school year even began, Monroe Township Schools in Williamstown, New Jersey, apologized to parents for placing books on its summer required reading list that included graphic descriptions of lesbian sex and a homosexual orgy, as well as recreational drug use. A committee of teachers, administrators, and librarians came up with the summer reading list, which was then approved by the school board, indicating that educators endorsed the content of the books.

• Despite abysmal progress on the core subjects that are necessary for a person to be considered nominally well-educated, students in the District of Columbia's fifth, eighth, and tenth grades took the nation's first standardized sex ed test.

Is it any wonder homeschooling has become such an attractive option for so many Christian families? A 2012 article from educationnews.org noted, "Since 1999, the number of children who are being homeschooled has increased by 75%. Although currently the percentage of homeschooled children is only 4% of all school children nationwide, the number of primary school kids whose parents choose to forgo traditional education is growing *seven times faster* than the number of kids enrolling in K-12 every year." (Emphasis added, because holy cow!)

But even homeschoolers can't escape the myriad cultural and political issues redefining our nation's character; they're just more obvious in the school setting. No matter how your children are educated, be ready to take advantage of teachable moments surrounding topics that require you to know and articulate your faith and values regarding a host of challenging subjects.

Ten Teachable Moments at School

> I believe in Christianity as I believe
> that the sun has risen; not only because I see it,
> but because by it I see everything else.
>
> —C. S. LEWIS

1. *The moment: Your children bring home notices that comprehensive sexuality education will be taught in all grades. You're uneasy about school-based sex education for your sixth and fourth graders, and you object to the idea that your kindergartner will have sex ed classes. How can you be sure the material is suitable for your kids, and what should you tell your children if you disagree with the material that is presented in the sex education curriculum?*

Christian parents who hope to instill their religious values regarding sex and sexuality should never allow a child to participate in any sexuality education class unless you have reviewed the curriculum and course materials in advance, discussed with the teacher how the lessons will be taught and in what format (single-gender classes,

PowerPoint presentations, videos, small group discussions, and so on). Having researched the program, you should also prepare your child by essentially preempting all of the instruction with conversations in your home about everything that will be taught at school.

If your research persuades you that the material to be presented in the classroom is not appropriate for your child for whatever reason, you should opt your child out of sex education classes. The laws about parents' rights vary from state to state with respect to consent to teach sexuality education, so you must become informed about the laws that impact your exercise of parental authority. The National Conference of State Legislatures lists the various state laws on its web site, ncsl.org (see this chapter's endnotes for the exact page). However, most laws are created to ensure you have the opportunity to know in advance that sexuality education will be taught, to review in advance the materials that will be used, and to opt out of the classes you deem inappropriate for your child. Bear in mind that most states *do* require at least a minimum amount of instruction on HIV/AIDS and sexually transmitted diseases as part of the mandated public health curriculum, and you can't opt out of some of this instruction.

It's fair to ask, why not just let your child participate in comprehensive sexuality education? After all, kids need information about human sexuality. They must know how and when their bodies will change, and everybody has to learn the essentials about "where babies come from." Besides, kids are surrounded by a hypersexual culture that assumes they understand and are interested in "sexy" media content. So wouldn't it make sense to let the school handle this, since it can be awkward to talk to kids about sex anyway?

No. The only way to both protect your child's innocence and provide information about sex and sexuality in the context of your faith and values is to teach it yourself, before the school district's progressive program—and the media, for that matter—have the chance to undermine the values you hope to instill on this crucial subject.

The healthiest and best way to teach children about sex is not to have "*the* talk" but to have *lots* of talks! In each age and stage of childhood, you will add new information—laden with your moral and religious values—so that your children are well-informed about sex and sexuality, but their innocence is preserved because you are teaching it all in the context of God's plan for human intimacy.

According to educator and author (and mom) Deborah Roffman, parents who speak openly to their children about sex become their child's "go-to" resource for information on this delicate subject. In so doing, these parents have greater influence on their child's decisions about sex. Kids whose parents are their primary resource for sexual information are likely to delay the onset of sexual activity and are more likely to adopt their parents' values about sex. But as Ms. Roffman notes in her book, *Talk to Me First: Everything You Need to Know to Become Your Kids' "Go-To" Person About Sex*, parents have to "get there first." Her advice is sound: You must assure that your child already knows all the information that might be taught in a sex education class.

So what to do when those notices come home about upcoming sexuality education classes? Start with an explanation to your children that goes something like this: "We know the school thinks it's important to educate kids about sex, but as your parents, this is our job. We're going to find out about the lessons plans and then we'll decide if the material is appropriate for you. Even if we choose to have you attend the classes, we're going to talk about the material you will learn at school so we can answer your questions and also make sure we explain things according to our faith and values. Sex is an important subject, and we want you to learn about it from us and feel comfortable talking to us about it."

Keep in mind that most of the kids at school will participate in sexuality education classes, and playground chatter about sex ed is still a thing, just like it was when we were children. Your preemptive formation on issues of sex and sexuality matters.

As your kids get older, you must be especially vigilant about the content of sex and sexuality lessons, because schools use prepackaged curricula that often go far beyond the objectives required by law. This is why you should not only ask about course content but also look over the materials that will be used in the classroom. Curriculum currently being taught in many states includes graphic explanations of heterosexual and homosexual sex acts, condom and vibrator demonstrations, and even presentations for high schoolers about pornography as sexual art. If you're not keen on your son or daughter sitting in a discussion that begins, "How would you feel if you had an intersexual child?" you need to pay close attention.

> **Sir, my concern is not whether God is on our side; my greatest concern is to be on God's side, for God is always right.**
> **—ABRAHAM LINCOLN**

2. The moment: Christmas season is approaching, and your third grader is excited to give handmade Christmas cards to her classmates. She draws pictures of the Baby Jesus in the manger, Mary and Joseph riding their donkey, and angels surrounding the newborn Savior. She makes enough cards for each classmate and signs them, "Celebrate the reason for the season!" But on the day she intends to hand them out, you pick her up from school and discover that her teacher would not allow her to distribute religious cards in the belief that they were offensive and illegal. Your daughter can't understand how sharing her excitement for Jesus's birthday could offend anyone, especially since all of the kids celebrate Christmas.

When it comes to religious suppression, a little ignorance goes a long way. Unfortunately, many well-meaning teachers and school administrators operate under the misguided notion that religious expression is not permitted in public schools, and that this includes any reference to religious holidays and symbols. Thus, public schools now host "Winter Concerts" right before the two-week break for "Snowy Season."

Examples abound of students across America whose constitutional rights to free speech and religious expression are squelched by public school districts that believe they are enforcing some sort of edict about separating church and state. Kids are told they can't wear crosses or religious jewelry, they can't include religious beliefs or themes in their papers or projects, and can't wear religious T-shirts to school. Districts ban Christmas carols and references to God at Thanksgiving, believing that they are following the letter and intent of the law. If only such a law existed, they'd be on target! All of these things are permitted under the US Constitution.

When a teacher or principal pronounces that you are violating the law, it's a brave family that stands up and says, "Not so fast." The Hickmans of Los Angeles are one such family. In February 2011, fifth grader Brian Hickman, Jr., auditioned for his school's annual talent show by dancing to one of his favorite Christian praise songs, "We Shine." A few days after his audition, a representative of the sponsoring PTA called Brian's mom, Adriana, to say he had done a wonderful job and was invited to perform, but asked that he choose a different song because his choice was too religious. Adriana called the principal, who further explained that Brian's song mentioned Jesus too many times. Meanwhile, the organizers had no problem with song lyrics of other participants that were sexual and suggestive, but I digress.

Adriana had a feeling the school wasn't allowed to restrict Brian's song choice in this way, but she wasn't sure. Referred to the Alliance Defending Freedom (ADF), she learned that students have a litany of rights to religious expression, and that nearly all of the restrictions placed on students by school officials and district policies are unconstitutional. Thanks to her bold choice to press the issue, and quick action by the lawyers of ADF, Brian Hickman won that battle. The Los Angeles Unified School District backed down, permitted him to dance to "We Shine" in the talent show—he was a huge hit, by the way—and most importantly, was reminded of the basic principles embodied in the First Amendment: religious liberty and freedom of expression.

Unfortunately, when schools misunderstand the law and misuse their power to make policy, one outcome is that children's civil rights are violated. Whether it's handing out Christmas cards or inviting classmates to an Easter egg hunt or a passion play, children have the right to share their faith as a way of engaging with others in their communities.

This teachable moment unfolds in two parts. First, explain to your daughter, "Sometimes people in authority make mistakes. Even though your teacher is a smart person and means well, she doesn't seem to know that you have every right to hand out your Christmas cards. You didn't do anything wrong, and we will work with the school to clear up this misunderstanding."

Then, do. There are great resources for parents to help advocate for your child's freedom of religious expression. Start at ADF's Web site (alliancedefendingfreedom.org, or see the bibliography for the specific page), and learn what's really true about religious expression in public schools. Then, when your child is unfairly restricted from free expression, speak up—confidently and respectfully—so that you demonstrate by your example that Christians are called to freely witness our faith.

Any time a school attempts to silence your child's expression of faith, you've been given the gift of a teachable moment promised to us by Christ himself, as recounted in Matthew 5:10: "Blessed are those who have been persecuted for the sake of righteousness, for theirs is the kingdom of heaven." No matter how young, our children can learn that speaking out for Christianity will always require the courage of their convictions.

I believe that unarmed truth and unconditional love will have the final word in reality.

—MARTIN LUTHER KING, JR.

3. The moment: Like all parents of school-aged children, you are concerned about the epidemic of bullying across the country. You are happy to learn that your child's school has implemented an anti-bullying education program aimed at empowering vulnerable kids, creating an atmosphere of intolerance to cruelty, and helping kids speak up and speak out on behalf of their peers. Your only concern: the program is laden with pro-gay language and themes. As a Christian parent, how do you respond when your child brings home materials about school safety that present homosexuality in a positive light?

It's ironic that the lobby for the gay agenda has literally bullied its way into the school safety movement by convincing Americans that anti-gay bullying is the most dangerous problem facing today's school children. To be sure, the media has alerted us to incidents in which gay kids are bullied because of their sexuality, and tragically, some of these cases have resulted in suicides. But bullying is not exclusive to gay students. Other factors are far more often the cause of the relentless and unfair treatment that some children endure at the hands of their peers.

What concerns many Christian parents is that the by turning this problem into a politically charged "bias" issue, schools now teach pro–LGBTQ values in ways that conflict with the moral and religious beliefs of many Americans.

Here's an example of this: In the 2009–10 school year, the Alameda (California) Unified School District (AUSD) adopted a school safety program that included a controversial segment known as "Lesson 9." In the first grade, AUSD's literature-based program would focus on the book *Who's in a Family?* by Robert Skutch ("Robin's family is made up of her dad, Clifford, her dad's partner, Henry, and Robin's cat, Sassy").

In second grade, students read *And Tango Makes Three* by J. Richardson and P. Parnell, the story of two male penguins, Roy and Silo, described as being "a little bit different" because "They didn't spend much time with the girl penguins, and the girl penguins didn't spend much time with them." When these male penguins hatch an egg, they decide, "We'll call her Tango because it takes two to make a Tango." The book claims, "Tango was the very first penguin in the zoo to have two daddies."

AUSD's third graders learn about the variety of family structures by watching a film called *That's a Family*, featuring some homosexual couples as well as traditional families. The curriculum also includes a list of LGBT vocabulary words that students must learn.

Parents in the AUSD objected, vocally and legally, by filing a lawsuit to eliminate "Lesson 9." They won, but only temporarily, as the court said the lesson wasn't politically correct enough. Since homosexuals are a "protected class," the lesson had to include other protected classes, such as racial minorities and people with physical disabilities. Once it was expanded to include these groups, the district was allowed to go forward.

Here's the interesting thing, though: bullying gay kids was not even an issue in the elementary schools of AUSD. Documentation from the district obtained by the Pacific Justice Institute (PJI) revealed that bullying due to homosexuality was not the problem. Most issues of bullying were based on sexual harassment and racial tension, not issues surrounding LGBTQ students. So teaching little kids about gay families is clearly meant to achieve some other objective.

More importantly, based on the prevalence of the problem, the issue of bullying isn't about who is being bullied; it's about the lack of conscience of too many of our nation's children to guide and inform their behavior. The Josephson Institute of Ethics survey I mentioned earlier found that half of all teens surveyed admitted they had bullied others, and nearly half—47 percent—said they've been the victims of bullying. So clearly, bullying goes far beyond LGBTQ empathy. It's a reflection of a moral vacuum in the hearts of young people.

If your elementary school's bully prevention program includes information about various kinds of families and relationships and seems to be promoting the homosexual lifestyle, you can tell your child something like, "It's true that families come in all shapes and sizes, and that some kids feel and act differently. The school wants you to understand how it feels for some kids who are different and who get bullied because of it. But we know that God calls us to love everybody and treat people with respect and kindness, because we are all his children. Bullying is always wrong. It doesn't matter why a kid gets picked on, it's never okay to bully someone, and it's not okay to stand by and let another person be bullied."

Middle and high school anti-bullying programs have grown more assertive in their efforts to instill empathy by normalizing homosexuality, even bringing in gay advocates such as the controversial and outspoken Dan Savage, founder of the It Gets Better Project. These presentations undermine any belief that God designs sex for a husband and wife, and instead teach a pro-gay worldview as unassailable fact. When your older kids are exposed to gay advocacy speakers, you are afforded an opportunity to discuss the cultural and political issues involved in the gay agenda, even as you support the anti-bullying message that the school is trying to send.

You might tell your child, "I am really glad the school is trying to confront the bullying problem, because in middle schools and high schools it is truly a dangerous and demoralizing issue. But you don't have to agree that homosexual behavior is okay to support and protect your gay friends. For that matter, you don't even have to like a person to protect him or her from being bullied. The moral thing to do is to look out for others who are vulnerable, even if you don't know them. So while it's great that the school wants to stop bullying, I think it's unfortunate that they're using it as a way to reinforce what some people believe about sexuality."

The key is to communicate openly with your child about the things that are being taught at school. Reducing bullying is a good goal. Using the bullying issue to promote the pro-gay agenda and challenge the tenets of the Christian faith is not cool.

> **The purpose of art is washing the dust of daily life off our souls.**
> —PABLO PICASSO

*4. **The moment:** Your daughter has been cast in her high school's upcoming production of the musical* **Legally Blonde,** *based on the movie starring Reese Witherspoon. She brings home the script and the two of you begin looking it over, realizing quickly that the stage version is racy, with salty language, sexual humor, and mature themes. You question the drama teacher's judgment for choosing a play that includes profanity and sexual humor. Your daughter wants to be in the show and doesn't want you to make a fuss about it, but you are uncomfortable with the material that will be acted on stage.*

This teachable moment is brought to you by the drama department at Loveland High School in Loveland, Ohio, where a 2012 production of *Legally Blonde* was cancelled and the drama teacher forced to resign after parents complained that the material in the show was improper for a high school musical.

It's not uncommon these days for high school drama departments to undertake plays and musicals that include profanity and portray mature, even disturbing, themes on the grounds that high schoolers are old enough to explore and present a broad range of topics. Some schools do this intentionally. In the spring of 2013, Shorewood High School in Shorewood, Wisconsin, launched a production of the Tony Award–winning musical *Spring Awakening*, which includes the topics of teen pregnancy, homosexuality, child abuse, sexual assault, and suicide. Principal Matt Joynt, who required students to present signed parental permission slips in order to audition, sent an email to parents saying,

> Given the content of the show, some may formulate questions regarding its progressive nature. Our goals for performing *Spring Awakening* are to produce a high quality and moving theatrical performance and to use the content of the show to encourage young people and adults to engage in dialogue about the real challenges our adolescents face. This is an opportunity to produce powerful theater and powerful conversation to support the young people we all serve.

It's fair to question this strategy, though, when you're talking about using the resources of the public school system to produce a play that some find offensive. To wit: The play *The Most Fabulous Story Ever Told*, a parody of Bible stories in which the characters are all gay, which was performed in 2013 at the Pioneer Valley Performing Arts School in South Hadley, Massachusetts. According to a HuffingtonPost.com news story, PVPA theater department director Mike Arquilla said, "In my opinion, those who find offense with this play will do so because they believe that homosexuality is a sin. At PVPA, we do not believe that to be the case."

Inconveniently, other folks aren't counting on Mr. Arquilla to define sin, as they believe God already has done so.

It's true, the arts offer myriad opportunities to focus on topics that challenge and even upset us. But many parents wonder what happened to the days when schools performed shows like *You're a Good Man, Charlie Brown*, and the raciest moment in a musical was Sister Sarah Brown's comic inebriation in *Guys and Dolls*.

If your school's drama department puts you on the horns of a dilemma, you may be faced with teaching the hard lesson: Sometimes we have to pass up an activity we enjoy in order to follow our consciences. If your research, including a conversation with the drama teacher, convinces you that the play will not be adapted to make it family-friendly, a tearful encounter may follow when you explain to your daughter that you don't support the school's decision to undertake a production that has teens cussing or acting out inappropriate scenes on the school stage.

If you decide your daughter cannot participate in the play, convey that decision with compassion. It's not her fault that the adults in charge chose a production that makes it difficult or impossible for some kids to participate. You might say, "I'm so sorry that the school's decision to do this play means that we can't support your participation. I know it doesn't feel fair to you. But as your parents, we have to make the decisions that we think are best, even when you don't agree with us—even when our decisions make you upset with us. That's okay. The point is, our values have to guide our choices, and the language and themes in this show don't reflect what we believe is appropriate for a high school play."

To be clear, it's not that the topics highlighted in controversial plays and musicals are off limits for high schoolers to discuss and understand. You should be openly talking with your teen about any topic, including the sensitive subjects highlighted in these productions. The issue is that productions for and by teens, meant to be performed for families and friends, ought not to compromise the actors or their audiences, especially when performed on a public school stage.

> **Courage is what it takes to stand up and speak; courage is also what it takes to sit down and listen.**
> —WINSTON CHURCHILL

5. The moment: Your daughter's high school science teacher injects her political opinions into the curriculum in ways that strike you as inappropriate. Though the class is Earth Science, the teacher spends little time on geology, geography, or soil science. Instead, she talks almost exclusively about ecology and the ways in which humans are "ruining" the earth through capitalism, with frequent

derogatory comments about corporations and business owners. Your family owns a business that employs hundreds of people, supporting their families and infusing your community with tax dollars. Your daughter has spoken up in class a few times to defend business owners and argue against her teacher's outspoken opinions, but she is afraid her grade will suffer if she continues to voice her point of view. How do you counsel a child whose teacher is overly political, and should you do something about it?

Teachers aren't required to check their First Amendment rights to free speech in the school parking lot—unless they want to speak about their Christian faith!—so students must learn to deal with a certain amount of political expression in the classroom, especially as they get to high school. This isn't necessarily a bad thing, because when a teacher expresses opinions contrary to your child's, she can learn to construct and articulate an argument and stand up for her beliefs. Good for her!

On the other hand, you have a reasonable expectation that your child's classroom will not become a hotbed of controversial politics, and that your child not be made to feel personally attacked by her teacher's outspoken opinions. Moreover, when a teacher's politics get in the way of tackling the course curriculum, your child's education is shortchanged. So it's key to know whether the expectations for instruction are being met, and if not, that is a problem you'd need to address.

We're living in a culture defined by political divisiveness, where folks think it's okay to turn nearly every issue and any conversation into an ideological battle, and the growing lack of civility that marks our public discourse is sadly creeping into areas where it most certainly does not belong. College and university classrooms now are well known as places where the political opinions of professors are deemed "fact." But these days, even high school and elementary school teachers share their opinions in ways that send the strong message to students, "My opinion is the only right answer." It's a skilled and reasonable teacher who can convey his or her opinions as "food for thought" without intimidating students into intellectual submission.

The issue becomes even more challenging in high school, when students often are assigned to read books that are blatantly anti-American or anti-capitalist. In 2011, one New Hampshire family felt they had no choice but to begin homeschooling their teen after he was assigned to read a book titled *Nickel and Dimed: On (Not) Getting By in America* by Barbara Ehrenreich, for a class on personal finance.

Parents Dennis and Aimee Taylor reviewed the book and concluded it is an anti-capitalist screed. More than that, the book contains offensive language, and even refers to Jesus Christ as a "wine-guzzling vagrant and precocious socialist." Digging deeper, the Taylors learned there weren't any books assigned for their son's class that would offer an opposing point of view, nor much on personal finance itself. Mostly, the curriculum for the class was leftist politics and economic opinion.

The Taylors' battle with Bedford High School resulted in a new law, passed by legislative override of a gubernatorial veto, which allows parents to provide, at their own expense, alternatives to public school curricula to which they object. Unfortunately, that option isn't available in every state.

As frustrating as it might be, an over-zealous and overly political teacher offers the opportunity to exhibit elements of strong character and learn some important life skills. You can encourage your child to be courageous, thoughtful, respectful, and reasoned as she formulates her responses to her teacher's comments. As you counsel her about how to handle the situation, you might say, "I know it's hard, but you can't take your teacher's opinion personally, especially if you want to make your side of the argument. You have to know your facts and be ready to share your beliefs without being rude or disrespectful." Use the time around the dinner table to talk about the issues raised in class, and to give your high schooler the chance to practice making her case.

Sometimes you just can't avoid meeting with a teacher, or even going further up the administrative ladder, to express concerns about antagonistic political arguments in the classroom. Students should never feel that they are being personally insulted or that their rights to speak freely are infringed, and when politics takes over a core subject like science, you're going to want to get the train back on the academic tracks before your child's education is compromised.

**If we ever forget that we are
one nation under God,
then we will be a nation gone under.**
—RONALD REAGAN

6. The moment: Your children let you know that they don't recite the Pledge of Allegiance to the flag at school. They do spend a fair amount of time studying multiculturalism and discussing "world citizenship," and the school devotes a full month, rather than just a day, to celebrating the earth. You believe public schools should help children develop a sense of pride, patriotism, and American citizenship. How can you use this situation to do just that in your kids?

This real life teachable moment comes from my local public school district, where I learned that the Pledge of Allegiance had been recited only twice a year: once during a flag raising ceremony in September, and once in June when the flag was formally taken down. Mind you, the flag went up and down every school day in between, but no one said the pledge. It wasn't until a concerned parent called the district to point out that state law requires the recitation of the pledge in public school classrooms each day that the practice was resumed. Sometimes, a phone call is all it takes!

As a culture columnist, I've noted for years the myriad ways in which our schools advance ideas about America that seem contrary to the patriotic sense of citizenship many of us feel for our country. From using the late Howard Zinn's controversial history textbook *A People's History of the United States* to promoting the idea that students are not citizens of a particular country but should think of themselves as "world citizens," the gradual acceptance of progressivism in public school curricula, and the political correctness it requires, means that American patriotism is often labeled "jingoistic."

How does this trend play out in our classrooms? And why should it matter to parents? Just ask the moms and dads of students in California who were suspended for wearing American flag T-shirts in May 2010, when the school was formally celebrating Cinco de Mayo. Or ask the folks in New York City whose five-year-olds were not permitted to sing "God Bless the USA" at their kindergarten graduation (but were allowed to sing Justin Bieber's "Baby"), because the principal declared the iconic Lee Greenwood song would be "offensive to other cultures."

Somehow, it was not deemed offensive that five-year-olds would sing a torch song by a hypersexual pop star. Go figure.

School districts now wrestle with the practice of reciting the pledge because atheist families argue it offends and excludes them, due to the words "under God." Of course, students aren't required to participate in the pledge—courts have ruled they can't be forced to speak the words. But placating the vocal minority that objects to the pledge has now eroded the sense that students share a common bond of loyalty to their homeland.

The dinner table is tailor-made for teachable moments about civics and society. When you use the dinner hour as a time to discuss and explore the events of the day, and also put issues and experiences from school in the context of your values, you'll be able to share your devotion to our great (I didn't say perfect!) nation.

Of course, this means you'll frequently explain that you disagree with some of what's taught at school. The trick is to express this in a way that doesn't undermine your child's respect for his teachers and administrators. Don't ever insult or demean an individual teacher, but rather explain your point of view about particular lessons, subjects, or school policies so that your child can learn to appreciate differing opinions and perceptions.

If your school is one that wavers on the pledge, talk to your child about what the pledge means and why it's important. You could also say, "I'm disappointed that your school doesn't have students say the pledge each morning, because I believe it's an important exercise in patriotism and citizenship. It's hard for kids to feel connected to their American heritage if it's not a part of their daily lives. Even if we aren't able to get the school to reinstate the pledge each day, I want you to understand how blessed we are to be American citizens and enjoy our freedoms." Make it a habit to talk about news stories and other events that allow you to discuss patriotism and your appreciation for our liberties and the people who protect them.

In our home, conversations about civics have always had a similar nature as those about media. Our aim was to educate and elucidate about the ways in which our values differ from what's being promoted outside our home, and to reinforce our children's understanding of citizenship in a traditional sense. Patriots come in all political stripes, and we appreciate that our kids may not ultimately share our politics, but instilling in them a love of country is the most important element to raising responsible citizens.

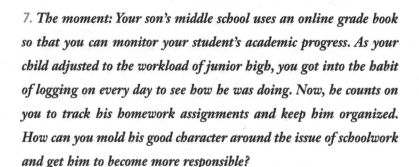

It's fine to celebrate success, but it is more important to heed the lessons of failure.
—BILL GATES

7. The moment: Your son's middle school uses an online grade book so that you can monitor your student's academic progress. As your child adjusted to the workload of junior high, you got into the habit of logging on every day to see how he was doing. Now, he counts on you to track his homework assignments and keep him organized. How can you mold his good character around the issue of schoolwork and get him to become more responsible?

Online grade books are both a blessing and a curse when it comes to helping our kids grow to become more responsible students and individuals. On the one hand, you can't help your child to succeed in school if you don't know what's going on, and there aren't very many middle schoolers who rush home to confess that they haven't done their literature assignments for the past two weeks. Usually, if you ask how school is going, you'll hear, "Fine. Do we have frozen pizza?"

Using online grade books to stay abreast of your child's progress is responsible on your part. But using them to do for your child what he should be doing for himself sabotages any developing sense of personal responsibility in your child. If you're checking the Internet every day to find out what the homework is, you're not metaphorically "teaching him to fish," you're serving fish sticks every night.

One reason parents become overly involved in managing schoolwork is that they are unwilling to let their children fail, or even to get a "C" on a test. None of us wants to see our children suffer for their poor decisions, but real and meaningful consequences offer compelling life lessons. "You'll feel really bad if you flunk the test" is called *fair warning*. Feeling bad when you flunk the test is called *regret*. And regret can be a strong motivator.

Now, to be clear, if your child is struggling academically, by all means work with his teachers, get a tutor, help him to learn systems that keep him organized, and use whatever tactics you believe are appropriate in order to get him to step up and work hard. But don't ever do the work for him. If you do, you'll teach exactly the wrong lessons: your grades are more important than your effort, and the perception you project to the world is more important than your integrity. Better an honest, responsible kid who does his best and gets lower grades than a child who learns to seek "success" at all costs.

From a parenting perspective, the issue raised here regarding online grade books is symbolic of a larger issue: "helicopter parenting." When moms and dads solve all of their kids' dilemmas, and arrange their lives to be smooth sailing and failure-free, they rob kids of some of the most essential life lessons. You can't learn to find solutions, make good decisions, fend for yourself, or rely on your wits if you never have the chance.

According to Indiana University psychologist Chris Meno, quoted in IU's online News Room, overprotective parents can produce offspring who are anxious, insecure, depressed, and incapable of independent decision-making. Meno counsels college students who are ill-prepared to take on the rigors of young adulthood because they've never had the chance to gain experience and confidence. She says the so-called protection of "helicopter parents" does more harm than good.

We put our kids on the path to independence when we separate from our children by giving them the space to make mistakes and solve their own problems. Teachable moments about independence and responsibility often present themselves in failure and disappointment at school. With every stinky test grade or sub-par report card, you can help your child to connect the dots between his conscientious effort and the outcome it produces.

If your child has grown dependent on you to monitor his school work (or to know where his soccer shoes are, or to bring his trombone to school when he forgets it), your teachable moment might go like this: "I know it's hard to juggle all the things you have to do, and

I can teach you some tricks to stay organized, but I'm not going to play the role of your personal secretary anymore. You have to learn to keep track of your homework and stay organized, and if you get bad grades because you don't stay on top of your responsibilities as a student, you'll suffer the consequences for that. So from now on, we're going to change the way we do things so you take responsibility for being a student."

Then, even when your son leaves his homework on the kitchen counter and you know he'll be downgraded for handing it in late, don't bail him out. Each time he slips, give him the gift of frustration and failure. The lessons in self-reliance are more important than the grades.

> **One test of the correctness of educational procedure is the happiness of the child.**
> —MARIA MONTESSORI

8. The moment: It's early in the school year, and already you're off to a rocky start with your daughter's second-grade teacher. She is an inexperienced educator, and you fear she has unreasonable expectations about active seven-year-olds. Each day at pick-up, you find yourself on the defense as the teacher complains to you about your daughter's "high-energy" behavior. You're worried you will be pressured to have her assessed for attention deficit disorder (ADD), with the goal of medicating her so that she'll fit with the teacher's vision of a calm, quiet classroom. So far, your focus has been on trying to get your daughter to behave, but begging, bribing, and threatening aren't working. Your little girl is losing her spark and says she "hates school."

If this scenario sounds awfully . . . *personal*, well, let's just say I'm a seasoned parent who has been there and done that. It took me years as a mom of school-aged children to understand that many great people choose the teaching profession, but that doesn't make them all great teachers. While some are gifted educators who have the knack for working with all kinds of children, others are simply not flexible or adaptive. Compounding the problem, young teachers don't have many tricks in the bag, so they count on parents to mold our sons and daughters to fit their expectations.

I've worked with all kinds of professional educators, some of whom clashed with my children. I learned that when you clash with a teacher, you must first determine if her expectations are unreasonable or if the problem is your child. To do this, you have to observe what's going on. Step one is to sit down with the teacher and say, "I'm worried we're off to a rocky start, but I'm committed to helping you, as well as helping my child. First, I need to see for myself what's happening in the school day." Commit to spending several full days in the classroom in order for the novelty to wear off for your child. (This might be a hardship for working parents, but an investment of two or three days in the classroom could save countless hours throughout the school year when you're called to teacher conferences because of problems at school. It might also be an important step to discovering a learning or developmental problem if one exists.) Be careful not to interact at all with your child—which means you must resist the temptation to correct or assist her. You're there to observe what's going on, not to fix it.

Teachers are allowed to have their own styles, and variations in teaching help to offer children a wide range of learning environments over the course of their education. But a teacher and student who just don't fit together can make for a difficult and unproductive year.

After you've seen for yourself what's happening in the classroom, you'll be in a better position to meet with the principal, and you'll have a stronger position from which to determine whether your child needs to be assessed for a medical condition like ADD. If you're satisfied that your child's behavior is age-appropriate, respectful, and obedient, and if your observations convince you that the atmosphere will never be right for her, she may need to be in a different classroom. In this "hypothetical" scenario, that's exactly what we decided for our daughter, because a little girl should never hate school or feel that her teacher doesn't like or care for her.

If you decide to make a change, present it to your child in positive terms. You can say, "You know what? We've decided to find a teacher who has more experience and can help you have a successful year. Your old teacher is a good person, but she doesn't seem to know how to work with us to help you to be successful. Your new teacher will be excited to have you in her classroom, and she'll understand how to help you do your best. I know it might seem hard at first to make a change, but I'm sure you will make friends in your new classroom and most importantly, you'll have fun learning. School is supposed to be fun and interesting, and we're going to make sure you are in a class where you can be your best and do your best."

It's important to present such a decision with confidence and enthusiasm, since your child is likely to be confused and even ambivalent about a change. Knowing that their parents are certain of their decision gives kids the trust and certainty they need to face a new situation.

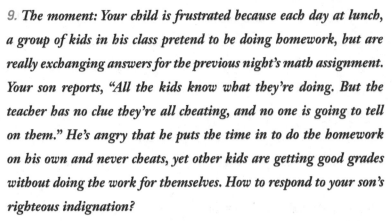

**Leadership and learning
are indispensable to each other.**
—JOHN F. KENNEDY

9. The moment: Your child is frustrated because each day at lunch, a group of kids in his class pretend to be doing homework, but are really exchanging answers for the previous night's math assignment. Your son reports, "All the kids know what they're doing. But the teacher has no clue they're all cheating, and no one is going to tell on them." He's angry that he puts the time in to do the homework on his own and never cheats, yet other kids are getting good grades without doing the work for themselves. How to respond to your son's righteous indignation?

It's small consolation to a kid who puts in long hours on algebraic equations that "cheaters never prosper," especially because, as he rightly notes, sometimes they do. (For a while, anyway.) The first and most important message is to remind your son how proud you are of his integrity and work ethic. You should say, "I realize that you could also take what looks like the easy way out and exchange answers with your friends, but you know that's wrong and unethical—not to mention, you won't learn math if you cheat on the homework." Knowing that you are proud of him for his solid character and consistent effort will be motivation for him to continue his good behavior.

Even if you're certain your child isn't cheating, it's always a good idea to revisit the subject when it comes up because somewhere down the line, cheating might seem like an attractive alternative. Kids cheat for different reasons—because they fall behind with homework, because they don't really understand the subject, or even because they're hyper-competitive and don't want to risk an imperfect score—so don't be surprised if your usually great kid gets caught cheating. (If you think this sounds like wisdom gained from personal experience, you'd be right.)

Whether it's the kids at school cheating or your own child who gets caught in the act, this is a crucial lesson in character that you must revisit time and again. You should stress that cheaters hurt themselves because they sacrifice their integrity for a perceived, short-term gain. They also hurt people around them; for example, the rest of the class that should get proper credit for honestly doing the homework. Most importantly, you want to draw the connection between cheating on homework while in school, and becoming a person who is comfortable cheating on other things in life. You could say, "One thing that worries me is that cheating can get to be a habit."

When this issue came up in our home, we grappled with the question, "Do you have a responsibility to tell the teacher that kids are cheating?" On the one hand, we're trying to raise children whose consciences lead them to right behavior and ethical action. On the other hand, no one wants to be the guy who rats out the cool kids for swapping answers to homework problems. It's like putting a sign on your locker that says, "Please stuff me inside." We agreed that one strategy might be to say privately to the teacher, "I'm not going to name names, but you might want to know that some kids are sharing their homework answers during lunch."

However, the essential message is that in life, people who make unethical or sinful choices always surround us, and we're called to set a moral example by simply doing the right things. It doesn't hurt to get an A in math, either.

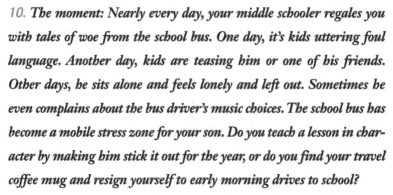

> My attitude is that if you push me
> toward something that you think
> is a weakness, then I will turn
> that perceived weakness into a strength.
> —MICHAEL JORDAN

10. The moment: Nearly every day, your middle schooler regales you with tales of woe from the school bus. One day, it's kids uttering foul language. Another day, kids are teasing him or one of his friends. Other days, he sits alone and feels lonely and left out. Sometimes he even complains about the bus driver's music choices. The school bus has become a mobile stress zone for your son. Do you teach a lesson in character by making him stick it out for the year, or do you find your travel coffee mug and resign yourself to early morning drives to school?

It used to be you could count on the school bus for two things: coming early on the days you were running late, and offering the perfect environment to learn a solid vocabulary of words spelled with only four letters. Now, we have MTV to teach profanity, and bus rides are sometimes recorded and posted on YouTube to shock us with evidence of children's behavior befitting animals in the zoo.

For the sake of argument, let's invent a statistic and decide that the atmosphere on school buses is perfectly fine 75 percent of the time. That means a quarter of the time the school bus is not providing a positive environment for your child. Is that reason enough to remove him from the bus and provide all of his transportation to school?

Maybe. Maybe not. It would depend on what your research tells you. To be sure, bullying is a serious issue, and you need to determine if your child is being victimized. A telephone call to the bus driver and transportation office with a request to watch the situation for a few days would give you some inside information about what's going on. Likewise, you'd want to speak to your child's teachers to understand the social atmosphere among your child's peers. If you determine your child is, in fact, being bullied, you most certainly would remove him from the bus and provide him with transportation—and moral support—to and from school every day, or find a suitable carpool.

On the other hand, if your research doesn't turn up a bullying problem, but rather reveals that your child is somewhat sensitive to the behavior of others, this teachable moment focuses you, appropriately, on helping your son to gain coping skills. This is part of "preparing the child for the path."

When it comes to exposure to profanity, I'm a fan of simple, factual explanations and definitions of slang. I never wanted my kids to use words they had heard but didn't know the meaning of, so when they asked about a swear word they had heard, I always defined it for them. As they got to be middle schoolers, I didn't wait for them to ask about words (because, let's face it, I didn't think they would), so instead, I would do a short but effective lesson in slang. Awkward? Absolutely. And also necessary unless you want your child asking you to "pass the [bleeping] potatoes" at the dinner table.

Importantly, when a child learns from you what slang and cuss words mean, he's less likely to be shocked and upset on the bus. You'll encourage him to ignore the kids who think it's cool to use foul language and pay attention to other kids instead.

It's important for kids to learn how to cope in uncomfortable circumstances, and if bus rides are good for anything, they certainly can be useful for this life lesson. You might strategize about how to make the rides more tolerable by cultivating "bus buddies" who are reliable friends, sitting closer to the driver, or listening to music on headphones. I'm not a fan of kids isolating themselves with ear buds, but it beats listening to a group of kids swearing on the school bus.

Your teachable moment might begin with a conversation in which you reassure your child that he can be brave and persevere even in a crummy situation. "I know the bus rides are frustrating to you, but I want you to be tough and learn to put up with unpleasantness once in a while. We all have to learn to have patience and perseverance when we're faced with situations that are annoying or difficult. Complaining about the bus isn't going to solve the problem, so let's think about how you might make it a better experience."

In our "helicopter parenting" culture, the first reaction many moms and dads would have is to pull their child off the bus, file an official complaint with the school district because their kid was made to feel uncomfortable, and then drive him to school each day, with stops at Starbucks along the way just to keep him cheery. That solution teaches the character traits of entitlement, self-centeredness, and emotional fragility.

If we want children who are brave, resilient, resourceful, and grow up to be problem-solvers, we have to give them some problems to solve. Riding the school bus is a great problem.

The Lesson Plan

We all want our kids' school experiences to be positive and encouraging, but school can present trials beyond just the rigors of academics or the emotional roller coaster of childhood friendships. The culture that saturates our media and influences our society generally is entirely present and powerful within the walls of our children's schools. How to use those encounters to your advantage? Here's the plan:

- *Stay a step ahead by talking openly with your child about sensitive or controversial subjects.* Be approachable, so that you'll be your child's first and most reliable source of information about personal, social, and cultural issues.

- *Use media stories about controversial issues to engage your child in important conversations.* Even if hot-button social issues haven't found their way to your child's school, you can talk to him or her about stories in the news that let you address topics that concern you.

- *Become a crackerjack researcher.* Remember that research is your first step, no matter how big or small the problem at school. Never assume you know the whole story. Get the info you need to make solid decisions on behalf of your child, as well as to instill the values and virtues that will mark your child's character.

- *Be involved.* The education of your children is your responsibility, not the school's. Staying involved is more than volunteering to be Class Mom or a parent coach; it means familiarizing yourself with curriculum and textbooks and assuring that you have appropriate input in decisions that affect your child.

- *Speak up when you're concerned.* As a parent, you have rights that must be respected by the school. Know your rights (or the policies if your child attends a private school) and exercise them when you feel there's a problem.

- *Remember that your primary responsibility is your child.* You might find yourself at the center of a storm if you challenge the school about an issue of concern. Some parents choose to fight battles publicly for the purpose of changing the system, but if you don't want to do that, it's okay. Just be sure you invoke your parental authority and advocate for your child.

CHAPTER SIX

Teachable Moments in Sports

IF YOU'RE LIKE MILLIONS of American parents, there's a good chance you're reading this book while waiting in a minivan or SUV for your son or daughter to emerge from sports practice. When you feel you're living the life of a team bus driver, sports psychologist, and athletic trainer, it might help you to know I wrote some of these pages in the high school parking lot while waiting for my cross-country runner to finish her workouts. You're not alone!

If America's family calendars are any indication, youth sports might be the central activity around which our time and priorities are organized. The National Alliance for Youth Sports (NAYS) reports that roughly 65 percent of our nation's youth play in organized sports programs, or about 35 million kids. From football Friday nights to weekend-long volleyball tournaments and every sort of athletic endeavor in between, much of our children's time is likely to be spent preparing for, playing, and recapping a game, meet, or match.

What's Healthy About Competition?

The benefits of playing youth sports have been well-documented. For example, high school athletes have higher grade point averages and are more likely to graduate than their peers who don't play sports. And the benefits to girls go beyond high school; playing sports increases the odds by 41 percent that a girl will go on to graduate from college. Also, the Women's Sports Foundation claims that female high school athletes are 80 percent less likely to get pregnant during their teen years than their non-athlete peers. Athletes aren't necessarily less likely to drink or engage in risky driving, but the incidence of drug use, as well as suicide and suicidal thoughts, is much lower among those who participate in high school sports.

Parents appreciate the benefits of sports for children, even for little ones who are still too young to master specific motor skills associated with a particular sport. Kids can get regular exercise, make friends, learn to follow directions, gain self-confidence, and build self-esteem by trying something new and feeing successful.

Many parents also enroll their children in sports programs to help them become more competitive, on the assumption that a competitive attitude will serve them later in life. Healthy competition is certainly a great venue to teach positive values, but the question is, what constitutes healthy competition?

It turns out most youth sports experts agree that until about age ten, children should engage in sports only on an instructional level, with little or no attention paid to scorekeeping or competition. One reason for watering down the rules and creating the false notion that "everyone wins" is because we're putting kids in competitive environments too soon. If the focus is on instruction, children aren't expected to exhibit the traits of a fierce competitor; rather, their aim is to learn the elements of fair play while understanding the rules and skills of an organized game.

When moving kids from instructional to competitive sports, it ought to be authentic. Ten-year-olds can't be fooled. They know full well that in every game, someone wins and someone loses. Rather than water down the atmosphere of competition, children must be taught to compete honorably, win or lose.

Measuring healthy competition is all about fun. If it's not fun, it's not healthy, and for children, participation is valued more than winning. Kids love playing games with their friends, working toward a shared goal, and celebrating when they're victorious. They also appreciate the efforts of their opponents and don't mind losing if the other team treats them with respect. Interestingly, a vast majority of kids say they would prefer to be on a losing team if they can play, rather than ride the bench for a winning team.

Some children exhibit a more pronounced competitive spirit than others, in the same way that some kids are naturally more or less outgoing, or musical, or artistic. A competitive spirit is innate and can't be taught; however, all kids must be taught *how to compete*, because in myriad ways, life will require them to do so.

When a Good Thing Goes Bad

Despite the positive outcomes associated with youth sports, NAYS says 70 percent of children who participate in organized sports during elementary school will discontinue their participation by age thirteen. What's the biggest reason kids quit sports?

It's not fun anymore.

More specific reasons can be gleaned from an overview of research about youth sports conducted by Michigan State University's Institute for the Study of Youth Sports (ISYS), which surveyed children's involvement, participation in, and dropping out from youth sports. The research found that the number one reason kids participate in sports is to be with their friends. When the focus of sports becomes competitive rather than social or developmental, the majority of kids preferred to disengage.

The research about youth sports has uncovered a disconcerting trend: the negative impact of adults—parents and coaches—on children's experiences in athletics. I can't prove this, but I think it's fair to say that when it comes to youth sports, every parent and coach knows what constitutes good adult behavior. Parents and coaches might say the focus is on fun and fitness, as well as positive experiences of competition. Yet this doesn't stop parents from hounding coaches about their kid's playing time, belittling their own children from the sidelines over missed shots or lax defense, or screaming obscenities at referees.

And while coaches often talk the talk of participation and developing players, their attitudes about winning at all costs are all too obvious to the children who never get to play in games, but instead are relegated to the practice squad.

Studies indicate many kids wish there were no parents watching them play sports, and disturbingly, one of the main reasons for quitting sports is the child's perception that coaches play favorites or are poor teachers. The hyper-competitive and overly emotional behavior of adults has now necessitated "sportsmanship contracts" that parents must sign in order for their kids to participate, outlining the expectations for children *and* parents.

If signed contracts seem like an unnecessary, even drastic, step, think about the cultural evolution around youth sports. It's alarmingly typical to see news stories about parents and coaches assaulting each other or verbally abusing officials. Invariably, the adults in these situations claim they acted on behalf of their children. It's a problem that seems to be escalating, despite efforts to get adults to set a positive example.

Consider a case from October 2013 that demonstrated intolerable adult behavior on a whole new scale: A father of a Florida youth hockey player was arrested for child abuse for allegedly going onto the ice to assault a fourteen-year-old player from an opposing team. The man said the targeted player had elbowed his son in a prior game, so the six-foot-three, 230-pound man punched the teen in the face, grabbed his helmet to slam his head against the boards, and had to be pulled off the child.

Admittedly, that's an extreme illustration. But you don't have to rush the ice to set a bad example. Adults undermine their children's athletic participation every time they bad-mouth a coach's decision, gossip about another player on their child's squad, or pressure their kids in ways that made them wish they weren't playing sports. When it comes to sportsmanship, adults can only teach by example.

Instilling "The Intangibles"

Youth sports began in our family when our eldest child, Kate, played in a first-grade instructional soccer league. We viewed her participation as successful whenever she stopped dancing on the field and noticed there was a game going on around her. When she was in the second grade, I asked her if she wanted to play soccer again. Her reply? "No, I did that already."

All four of our children played various sports through the years, including basketball, soccer, baseball, and softball. They all eventually chose cross-country running and track as their high school sports, and our son took his talent and love for these sports to the next level, competing in a Division I college program.

I couldn't guess the cumulative miles my four children have run since Kate first joined the cross-country team in 2003, but I know one thing for certain: even for my college athlete, what my children have learned through their sport has almost never been about running or racing. It's always about becoming the person God calls them to be. In sports lingo, the traits they have developed are known as "The Intangibles"—the inherent character that ultimately defines an athlete's essential nature.

Sports clichés aside, there's no question that athletic competition works as a perfect metaphor for life. In the course of a sports contest, an athlete experiences the full range of trials, tribulations, and triumphs that everyone faces from time to time. Sports create countless opportunities for personal decision, such as the moment when an athlete either gives up and accepts a loss, or perseveres until the end in pursuit of his or her best effort. Decisions like these build character. In the long lens of parenting priorities, winning or losing is never the point. Instead, the more our children can experience first hand the pride, disappointment, determination, and cooperation required to achieve an objective, the more likely they are to internalize the life lessons that matter most. Years after our children have grown up and left their athletic careers on the pages of their high school yearbooks, the personal qualities discovered through sports will mark them as adults.

Children don't have to be good at sports to gain from the experience. I'm convinced that the times my kids struggled in sports were more valuable to their character than the (admittedly fun) times when they were successful. No matter what his or her level of athletic participation, every child can internalize these elements of good character through sports:

- *Integrity.* Fair play is the cornerstone of sportsmanship, so exhibiting personal integrity is the mark of a true competitor. Winning and losing are meaningless without honor. Teaching kids to value honesty and fair play in sports is a lesson that can and should permeate all other aspects of their lives.

- *Poise and maturity.* Staying focused under pressure and rising to the occasion when pressed to do one's best are lessons that extend far beyond the field of play. Through sports, athletes have the chance to develop habits of self-discipline and composure that are useful in every area of life.

- *Perseverance.* Sports provide an opportunity to learn the virtues of diligence and determination in the face of a difficult task. The work ethic required in athletics offers the chance to learn that dedication over time is usually the only way to achieve one's goals. In a culture that stresses instant gratification as a standard for happiness, learning the value of perseverance can mold a child's character and inform his or her faith.

- *Humility.* Team sports invariably include athletes of all abilities; thus, both superior athletes and those who are less skilled can learn the virtue of humility. Kids who are naturally more gifted in sports can grow as leaders and inspire others to do their best, while less accomplished kids can learn to appreciate the talents and contributions of others and set the positive example of team spirit.

- *Grace.* Exuding grace no matter the outcome is the definition of sportsmanship. Winning and losing are equally meaningful experiences when kids learn to be gracious winners and to exhibit courtesy and respect through a loss.

These traits are not only essential in some distant future but will serve children in their daily lives as they grow up in an ever more challenging culture.

Of course, not every child is interested in sports, but these life lessons can be gained from any sort of extracurricular activity. Music, dance, art, STEM clubs, debate teams—you name it!—all offer opportunities to learn new skills, engage in healthy competition, test one's mettle, and grow in character and maturity. There's no limit to the ways in which we can help kids to practice the virtues that will serve them now and throughout their lives.

That being said, let's look at some common teachable moments in sports, and how you can use them to instill character in your children.

Ten Teachable Moments in Sports

There are only two options
regarding commitment.
You're either in or you're out.
There is no such thing as life in-between.

—PAT RILEY

1. The moment: You enrolled your daughter in tennis lessons during the summers when she was very young. She was a natural. Through the years, she turned into an exceptional player, climbing the ranks in junior tennis. She always loved the sport and the friends she made traveling around the state. Her involvement in travel tennis has been a focus for your family for several years. But now, as she approaches high school, she tells you she's not interested in playing tennis and instead plans to try out for golf and run track. You can't believe it! Her talent could take her far—perhaps get her a college scholarship—if only she sticks with it and works hard for the next four years. After thousands of dollars in private lessons and travel, should you require her to play tennis in high school?

In our youth sports culture, the phenomenon of "child pros" is not uncommon. Organized far beyond the confines of local communities, programs for hockey, soccer, basketball, baseball, tennis, and swimming operate like professional leagues, with year-round training and travel through the state, region, and nation for tournaments and championships. The requirements for these programs include hefty fees and the expectation that families will travel along with the team for competitions.

Parents of kids who participate at this level often give up their own interests and even tailor their jobs to accommodate their children's athletic "careers." These folks admit they have little by way of a personal life beyond carting their kids to practices and competitions, and their friends tend to be the parents of other kids involved in their programs. So it's easy to see why parents would feel personally invested in their children's activities and are conflicted if their kids decide to quit their sport and change directions. Some feel their investments of time, money, and emotional support entitle them to demand that their children stick with a sport. Others might label the decision a "waste of talent," especially if kids have the potential to be successful on a larger stage. Perhaps without intending it, the trophies and medals earned by their children become vicarious accomplishments for moms and dads.

For these reasons and more, everything I've read about "child pros" warns of the risks to kids of being involved at this level. They can experience emotional burnout, physical injury, and even depression and drug abuse because they feel "locked in" to an activity that defines them and overtakes their young lives. Experts say that rather than prepare kids to take their talent further, participation at this level can backfire, resulting in kids who reject the sports in which they excelled because they resent the pressure and loss of carefree childhoods.

But even if a child's participation in a sport isn't at the "child pro" level, it's common for parents to be overly invested in the activity. Many overestimate their kids' athletic abilities and prospects. Ask any high school coach who's had to field phone calls from angry parent about playing time. American parents do not suffer from a lack of confidence in their kids. That bias persuades many parents that their children are uniquely talented and are destined for college scholarship offers.

But according to the National Collegiate Athletic Association, only two percent of high school athletes are awarded athletic scholarships in college! Many of those scholarships are only partial awards for books or tuition. The vast majority of students who compete at the college level do so for love of the sport. Beyond college, the odds of becoming a professional athlete are miniscule. The NCAA reports only about 1 percent of college athletes go to the pros in basketball (men's and women's), football, men's ice hockey, and men's soccer. A whopping 9.7 percent of college baseball players go to the majors, but that represents fewer than 700 NCAA players per year. All in all, planning to be a pro athlete is like planning to win the lottery, only sweatier.

Regardless of their natural talent, children who are committed to a sport or activity don't need much encouragement to stay engaged.

You can't force passion! If your child has it, you're likely to be flashing the lights on the driveway to get a basketball player to come in for the night, or asking a musician to turn down the volume while the family enjoys a show on TV. No matter how accomplished a child is in a sport or activity, the desire to do it has to come from within and can't be borne of guilt or pressure.

When a child's activity is the focal point of a family's time and resources for many years, she may believe she isn't free to give it up for fear of disappointing you. Kids can forget that we love them unconditionally, and that our support for their activities is an expression of that love. When we give them the freedom to walk away, we remind them that it was never about the sport or activity; it was always about what their participation could teach them about character, conscience, and faith.

So even if you've spent a considerable amount of time and money on a sport or activity, it's crucial for you to keep the focus on personal development. If an activity helps your child to gain poise and confidence, exhibit grace under pressure, compete with integrity, and use her or her God-given talents in ways that are wholesome and benefical, and if it's something your child *wants* to do, follow her lead as far as you're willing and able to support her ambitions.

But if she wants to give up a longtime activity, be open to her feelings. Listen and learn why. The goal here isn't to teach her that she's obligated to pursue a particular dream, but to learn to make wise choices about how she spends her time and energy. You might say, "You've invested so much effort into this, so you must have given it a lot of thought. Tell me how you got to this decision." Perhaps she wants to explore different interests before the chance is lost, or is tired of the routine or demands on her schedule. Maybe she just wants to live like a "normal" kid, especially in high school. No matter what she says, don't try to convince her to stick with it. Instead, encourage her to pray about her choice and give her the freedom to do what she really wants to do.

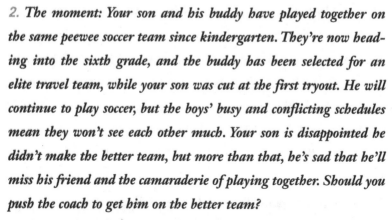

Never give up!
Failure and rejection are only
the first step to succeeding.
—JIM VALVANO

2. The moment: Your son and his buddy have played together on the same peewee soccer team since kindergarten. They're now heading into the sixth grade, and the buddy has been selected for an elite travel team, while your son was cut at the first tryout. He will continue to play soccer, but the boys' busy and conflicting schedules mean they won't see each other much. Your son is disappointed he didn't make the better team, but more than that, he's sad that he'll miss his friend and the camaraderie of playing together. Should you push the coach to get him on the better team?

It's a reflection of our ultra-competitive sports culture that kids are grouped by ability at such young ages. Children grow and mature at different rates, so it's shortsighted at best to focus on the kids who happen to hit puberty earlier, and therefore are bigger, faster, and stronger than others. Eventually, everybody catches up, but by then, the die is typically cast and the so-called elite athletes are already identified. It's a practice that suits the coaches who care more about winning than bringing kids along, but these are the times in which we live.

Being cut from a team might have social consequences, but it's a bad idea to try and lobby a child onto the roster just so he can keep playing with his friends. Even if you were successful, the experience would likely be more negative than positive. The coach wouldn't really want your child on the team, and making the elite team would not assure that your son had the chance to be involved and have fun. While kids care more about being with friends than being on a "better" team, coaches who seek out only the best players have made their priorities obvious.

As much as we'd like to protect our children from heartache when they're cut from a team or activity, or when their participation doesn't turn out to be what they expected, experiences of disappointment present opportunities for parents to teach and children to practice the attributes of sportsmanship that ultimately make for the most coachable kids. Down the road, the ability to process disappointments will serve a child well if he misses out on admission to a particular college, or isn't hired for a "dream" job. Everyone must learn to pick himself up, dust himself off, and keep going, and you only learn that response through hard experience.

If your child is cut from a team or activity, fight the natural urge to express anger at the folks who cut him. It may be a natural response, but it doesn't help the child, who only wants to be comforted and reassured that things will work out. Instead, say, "I know how disappointed you are, and believe me, I am disappointed for you. And I know you're worried about how you'll stay friends with your buddies on the team. But we will make sure you have chances to hang out together, and even though you might not believe this now, you'll make new friends on your new team. The important thing about soccer is playing and having fun, and that's still something you can do. But yeah, it stinks to get cut."

It helps if you can tell your kids a parallel story from your childhood, or can point to a similar experience of a sibling, friend, or relative. Also, ice cream helps. Always get ice cream when a kid gets cut from a team.

When you come to a fork in the road, take it.
—YOGI BERRA

3. The moment: Your four children are involved in a host of activities. One is an accomplished dancer, another plays golf and tennis, another is emerging as an excellent soccer player who also loves basketball, and the youngest is involved in instructional classes of all kinds. You're pleased that your kids enjoy their activities, but your life now revolves around them six days a week. Your afternoons are spent driving from practices to lessons to games, with quick stops at home for frozen dinners and frequent fast food meals on the run. What began as a well-intentioned effort to expose your children to different opportunities for enrichment, fun, and exercise has become an exhausting and deflating lifestyle. Family meals take place only on weekends, and only if there's nothing else to conflict with a sit-down dinner. Is this just a season in life that must be endured, or can you—and should you—adjust your priorities as a family?

It is mindlessly easy to allow our family calendars to turn into Excel spreadsheets of adolescent activity with few open spaces for downtime, much less dinnertime. What might seem manageable with one or two children becomes unwieldy with three or more. Yet, in larger families, parents often feel obligated to allow younger children the same opportunities that their older kids enjoyed.

Fair enough. But the fact remains: there are only twenty-four hours in a day, and only seven days in the week. If each child engages in two or three activities per week that require multiple practices, lessons, and competitions, you're looking at up to a dozen different programs, each with its own time commitments and expense.

Executing this kind of lifestyle requires compromises, and some of those aren't good. For example, in order for you to get three kids to their various lessons and practices, your fourth child may spend the afternoon in ear buds, passing the time with movies on an iPad. (Could we all agree a child's time is better spent playing outside, reading, having a friend over, or walking the dog?)

Shuttling through town, you're likely to feed the kids in shifts, and often from a drive-thru, or else dole out snacks to hold them over for a hastily prepared dinner eaten late in the evening. Homework is done after an already-exhausting twelve-hour day, and "downtime" is defined by an hour of TV before bed.

Oddly, though, parents don't seem to think twice about catering to their kids' many activities, especially if those activities can be described as *elite*. It's almost a cliché to hear parents walk across a parking lot after a soccer or hockey game, comparing notes about their busy schedules with words like *crazy* and *out of control*, yet they're obviously proud, because the frenetic pace of their lives is somehow a reflection of their children's wonderfulness. It's competitive parenting on a scale that goes from "vicarious achievement" to "weirdly obsessed." Is this our new normal?

Raise a hand if you're a little bit guilty of overextending your kids' activities. (Note: my hand was up while I typed that sentence.) It's almost impossible not to find ourselves at the mercy of our calendars and the many "important" and "valuable" opportunities available to our children. After all, you wouldn't sign them up if the activities weren't good for them, right?

Even if you start with reasonable policies about what you'll permit—say, each child can choose one sport per season and one arts or enrichment class—you realize in short order that the older your kids get, the more things they want to pile onto their plates. One kid gets the lead in the school play. Another is asked to join an off-season, indoor soccer team. Your daughter's Girl Scout troop ups the ante on cookie sales, and your high school freshman announces she's been selected for a competitive musical ensemble that meets during "Zero Hour."

Suddenly, even the hours before dawn require a carpool.

"Important" and "valuable" as these opportunities may be, they come at a steep and lasting cost. The most devastating impact of all this activity on the American family and on the personal character and well-being of our nation's children is the loss of family dinners as an expected and protected ritual. As much as we'd like to believe that our frenetic schedules benefit our children, when they eliminate the opportunity to sit down as a family several times each week to share a meal, they're doing more harm than good.

I'm not trying to make anyone uncomfortable or lay a guilt trip on conscientious and hard-working parents who are only trying provide their kids with rewarding, active lifestyles. I realize that pulling the plug and declaring that family mealtimes will now take precedence over all of your kids' extracurriculars may feel like an impossibility. Yet I have friends who gathered their brood together one afternoon—a day their kids refer to as Black Sunday—and announced the decision that they would take a full season off. The response was predictably emotional, but that homeschooling family determined they needed time for togetherness and adventure.

We all say we want what's best for our children. Every sort of study, and they are legion, concludes that children who eat family dinners multiple times per week achieve better outcomes in a wide range of measures than do kids who don't have frequent family meals. And one of the most recent studies published in the *Journal of Adolescent Health* in 2013 says the more family meals per week, the fewer emotional and behavioral problems, and the more positive relationships and happiness. In the case of family dinners, more is better.

It's hard to defend sacrificing something this reliably beneficial to your children's well-being for a life that is affirmatively more stressful, hectic, exhausting, and expensive. What's wanted is balance, and conveniently, teaching our children to live a balanced and healthful lifestyle ought to be one of our parental goals. Finding the right balance between a healthfully active schedule and protected family time may require sacrifices, but the overall picture should be one of stronger family bonds and more satisfaction with the things each person ultimately chooses to pursue.

Teachable moments present themselves each time a new opportunity arises to begin an activity, as well as each new season when it's time to sign up for teams and sports programs. Rather than slide into an overextended schedule, call a family meeting to evaluate everyone's commitments and the impact they have on the family dynamic. It might be shocking to hear that your kids don't want to continue an activity that you assumed they preferred. When confronted with the choice between a breathtakingly busy life and the chance to hang at home three afternoons a week, play outside until dark, and have dinner as a family, your kids may make it easy to re-prioritize.

Start the meeting by saying, "We've taken a long, hard look at our calendar and we've decided we have to cut some things in order to live a more balanced life. We need to make family dinners a priority, and we also need to leave open space on the calendar to just hang out, play, and relax. Everyone needs the chance to do the things they love to do, but let's see what our schedule would look like if we cut out a few things." Kids need to know that you appreciate their sacrifices if cutting the activity list means giving up something they enjoy. And you need to reassure them that they can make different choices down the road.

This is what it means to be a leader of your family. Moms and dads who are "victimized" by their kids' busy schedules are actually letting their lifestyles—and their relationships!—be defined by soccer coaches, dance teachers, martial arts instructors, and the whole host of folks who get more of your children's time than you do. Taking control of the schedule and asserting your authority to protect family mealtime will send a strong and positive message about what matters most.

> **Most people run a race to see who is fastest.
> I run a race to see who has the most guts.**
> —STEVE PREFONTAINE

4. The moment: Your daughter signed up for the cross-country team at school. She loves the kids on the team, but hates running. Most of the other kids have been doing the sport for a while and are already in shape. Your daughter is improving but still lags behind, so she spends many of the practices running alone. The season has barely begun, but she complains constantly and begs you to let her quit the team. Should you force her to stick it out or let her walk away? What's the point in making her do it if she's miserable?

This question comes up for almost every parent at one time or another. If it's not a sport, it's piano lessons, marching band, tae kwon do, or competitive dance. Typically, it involves something that started with your child's enthusiastic promises to practice and participate, convincing you to cough up a large outlay of cash. But invariably, it devolves into a steady stream of whining, complaining, bickering, and tears.

You really can't claim your parenting chops until you've handled this classic conundrum.

I think the problem is cultural, at heart. In our commercialized society, children respond to compelling advertising, so the promise that something will be fun may persuade them to pursue a particular activity. But kids don't look past that nebulous promise of future "fun" to evaluate an activity's true requirements. If their friends are running cross-country, or the dance recital costumes are cool, or they like the idea of breaking a board with one chop, they'll commit. Hard work? Long hours at practice? Rehearsals marked by tedious repetition? No worries.

Parents know better. Learning a new skill or taking up a new sport is an inherently challenging pursuit. If you've never run a mile without stopping, the idea that you are expected to run for forty continuous minutes might make you cry before you even lace your shoes. So before you have a discussion with your child about quitting a new-found activity, make sure he has given it enough time to conquer at least a portion of the learning curve.

Of course, some kids and some activities are simply not a fit. It may be too difficult to break into the social structure that already exists, or perhaps a coach or instructor is more intense than he or she seemed. Some things just aren't as much fun as they appeared they would be. Fair enough. But is that a reason to quit?

Generally, the best life lesson a child can learn in these situations is to persevere until the end of the season (or the conclusion of your prepaid lessons, and so on). Quitting may seem to your child like the fastest and easiest route to happiness, but it may not be the most effective route. She may need to learn that happiness shouldn't always be our immediate goal—that sometimes, the route to happiness is pride in tackling a difficult task. Sometimes happiness is the genuine self-esteem discovered by getting better at something over time. Sometimes, it's merely keeping a commitment, no matter how hard. You get the drift.

There are as many teachable moments in this scenario as there are ways to complain about cross-country practice. One day, you might say, "I get that it's hard. That's why I'm so proud of you! Just take it a day at a time." Another day you might say, "Do you realize how much you're already improving? Two weeks ago, you couldn't do what you did today." The next day you could say, "Complain all you want. I'm impressed with you!"

There may be a day when you reach your limit for positive reinforcement. On that day, consider saying, "If you complain about this activity one more time, I'm signing you up again. Period. End of discussion. If you want the freedom to make different choices in the future, I suggest you learn what it means to be mature in the face of a difficult challenge and stop complaining." I would throw in a line or two about children who would give anything to have the chance to participate in activities, including kids whose parents can't afford to sign them up, and those who are physically unable. But then again, Catholic guilt is not just a stereotype. We really use it to help mold a working conscience.

One man practicing sportsmanship is far better than fifty preaching it.
—KNUTE ROCKNE

5. The moment: Despite regular reminders about sportsmanship, including an announcement at the start of every eighth-grade basketball game noting the expectations for fans in the stands, the father of your son's teammate continues his bombastic outbursts, causing untold embarrassment to his son and everyone else in the gym. This otherwise nice guy is a caricature of a boorish sports dad—

loud, gruff, rude, and humiliating. Whenever his son is in the game, his sideline "coaching" cannot be ignored. It is heartbreaking to see his son's slumped shoulders and dejected sighs each time he returns to the bench. Your son has even mentioned how badly he feels for his buddy. What should you say to your son about the behavior of this adult? And should you make an issue of it by complaining about this dad to the school principal and athletic director, or just endure his rude outbursts until the end of the season?

There's probably nothing more confusing or disturbing at a youth sporting event than watching adults belittle and antagonize others from the sidelines. Whether it's a parent yelling critical comments at his son or daughter, or a coach using negative words to "motivate" his team, or anyone yelling at the officials, the prevalence of bad behavior on the part of grown men and women will pepper your child's athletic experiences with examples of poor sportsmanship that will serve as teachable moments.

There's no excuse for adults to be so caught up in a child's game or competition that they can't control their emotions or behavior, and yet surveys indicate this remains a serious problem. According to a September 2013 study released by Liberty Mutual Insurance's Responsible Sports program, the 501 coaches surveyed say it's common for parents to exhibit bad behavior. Fifty-five percent report that parents yell negative things at their own children, 44 percent say parents yell at or insult officials, 40 percent have seen parents yell at other children, and 39 percent say parents shout negative comments at coaches. That's not a small fraction of the folks in the stands!

But these statistics aren't nearly as compelling as the dejected look on a child's face when he's belittled by his dad or mom on the sidelines. A child who is so rattled by his parent's screaming that he can't focus on the game, or who retreats to the bench fighting back tears, is in need of compassion, and perhaps an advocate in the gym.

In situations like this, when your child feels powerless to help a friend, the most important message to reinforce with him is that we're never powerless. We always have the power of prayer at our disposal. Remind your son that praying for his teammate and his father is a concrete, useful, and potent response.

You can also encourage your child to reach out and support his teammate. You might say, "It must not be easy for your buddy to concentrate on the game with his dad yelling at him. I hope you let him know that he's doing fine. Some parents put a lot of pressure on their kids to do well in sports, but what's important is that he knows you and the rest of the guys appreciate him." It can't hurt to give your son the information about kids' motivation to play sports—it's to hang out with their friends. Remind your son to be a friend, first and foremost.

The bad behavior of adults opens the door for a frank conversation with your child about the culture around kids' sports. Ask your son his opinions about the way parents and coaches have interacted with him during his sports experiences. Parents are often shocked to know how their "support" is perceived from across the court. If you're like me and you've occasionally been overly enthusiastic (though not negative) in your sideline cheering, you may need to apologize and promise to never again be the loudest mom in the stands. Most importantly, use a conversation about the overall sports culture to emphasize your beliefs about the value of sports for fun and learning.

Finally, there's the question about whether you should take on the role of advocate for the boy on your son's team whose dad is loud and negative. Doing so can be an effective way to demonstrate to your child, by your example, that we are all sometimes called to protect and advocate for others, even in small and subtle ways. You could explain to your son, "We parents ought to be as invested in promoting good sportsmanship in the stands as we are in teaching our kids to act accordingly, so I feel like I ought to speak up. I may not talk directly to that dad about his behavior, but I'm going to mention it to the coach or athletic director. If they hear from another parent that it's making us uncomfortable, perhaps they'll ask him to calm down."

Sadly, our kids must learn that bullying is an issue even for adults. A man who's an obvious bully and who belittles his child in public ought to be reported for no other reason than to alert school officials of your concern.

> **Sportsmanship for me is when a guy walks off the court and you really can't tell whether he won or lost, when he carries himself with pride either way.**
> —JIM COURIER

6. *The moment: Your high school freshman is a sore loser. After every loss, he gets angry and emotional. If you try to comfort him or put a positive spin on things, he becomes argumentative and blames his teammates for playing badly, while claiming that he is the only*

one who does what he's supposed to do. He's obnoxious! How can you get him to lighten up and have fun, win or lose?

This is one of those times I'm glad my son has good self-esteem and a great sense of humor, because I'm about to reveal that I wrote this question based on a vivid mental image of my Jimmy, at fourteen, fussing and fuming after soccer and basketball games in which his teams went down to defeat. He was such a sore loser he made road rage look reasonable. He got mad when he landed on the short end of the score in driveway hoops with his buddy Jon. He got mad when losing at gin rummy and chess and bowling. Come to think of it, he'd get mad if he lost on a wishbone. Jimmy really hated to lose.[1]

No one likes losing, but learning to do so gracefully is one of the most essential lessons to be gained from participation in sports. Because let's face it: life offers lots of opportunities to find yourself on the losing side. Why not do it well?

It takes some kids a while to get this grace. Adolescent boys, in particular, typically lack the maturity to accept defeat without responding emotionally. Simply waiting until they outgrow their emotionalism isn't a great answer, since habits and attitudes are shaped during those formative years. Also, if losing gracefully is the sign of good character, being a sore loser is a sign you haven't developed much of what matters most: a sense of fair play, respect for an opponent, or humility.

It's easy to get trapped into an argument with a fussy teenager

---

[1] Hotheaded adolescent behavior recounted with permission from the perpetrator. Also, Jimmy's obnoxious phase didn't last long! He quickly grew into a gracious competitor known for showing genuine respect for his opponents.

about what happened in a game or competition. You want to focus on the larger issue of sportsmanship or emotional maturity, but you find yourself bickering about whether the ref could see that a player was offside, or whether the shot got off before the buzzer. These disputes are filed under: "Pointless." Engaging in them only allows a sore loser to wallow in his immaturity.

I'm always a fan of the heart-to-heart chat, and you could certainly go that route. But in our culture, we spend a lot of time analyzing kids' feelings and validating their emotions. In this case, I think we could all agree that it feels bad to lose, but this doesn't mean it's okay to be obnoxious. Kids who can't demonstrate a cheerful attitude when they lose quickly discover that no one wants to play with them.

If you've tried the heartfelt chat, patience, cajoling, humor, and diversions to get your child to work through his anger about losing, it may be time to lay down a new law. There's a place in the world for "Zero Tolerance," and poor sportsmanship is it. Say something like, "You're allowed to feel your feelings, but you are no longer permitted to express them in a way that shows me you're a sore loser. Learning to lose gracefully is more important than winning, and if you can't show me you're capable of playing and accepting the outcome of a game—win or lose—with equal grace and humility, you're getting benched." Then, give your kid one more chance to demonstrate that he understands your new rule. If he acts out again, call the coach and explain that you have benched your son for a game to teach him a life lesson about managing his emotions and behaving with greater maturity. You should only have to do it once before you see marked improvement!

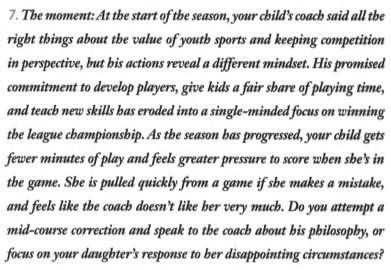

Do you know what my favorite part of
the game is? The opportunity to play.
—MIKE SINGLETARY

7. The moment: At the start of the season, your child's coach said all the right things about the value of youth sports and keeping competition in perspective, but his actions reveal a different mindset. His promised commitment to develop players, give kids a fair share of playing time, and teach new skills has eroded into a single-minded focus on winning the league championship. As the season has progressed, your child gets fewer minutes of play and feels greater pressure to score when she's in the game. She is pulled quickly from a game if she makes a mistake, and feels like the coach doesn't like her very much. Do you attempt a mid-course correction and speak to the coach about his philosophy, or focus on your daughter's response to her disappointing circumstances?

Hearing all the "right things" generally means parents are reassured that a coach will care about their child's personal experience on the team, and that the level of competition will be appropriate for the age of the kids in the program. But it turns out parents and coaches may not even be speaking the same language when they discuss their respective expectations about an upcoming season.

In addition to surveying coaches, the Liberty Mutual Insurance Responsible Sports survey (mentioned above) also included one thousand parents whose answers to survey questions revealed the inherent conflict between parents' and coaches' priorities. For example, 77 percent of parents put a high priority on their child's coach being a caring person, versus only 59 percent who put the same priority on the coach being skilled in that sport. Three out of four parents said the reason they enrolled their child in sports was to have fun. (Still, 36 percent of coaches said they've had problems with parents' unreasonable expectations about winning!)

Overall, the importance of competitiveness in youth sports was greater for coaches of children in all age groups than for their parents, and the disparity was most pronounced for elementary-aged kids, with 76 percent of coaches saying competitiveness was important, versus only 56 percent of parents.

What's needed is a coach-to-parent dictionary. When a coach says he wants the kids to have a "positive experience," he may mean he wants them to be on a winning team and know what it feels like to work together to achieve a shared goal. When parents say this, they often mean they want their child to actually play, occasionally score, and smile—win or lose—because she's having fun with her pals.

If your child is stuck in the middle of a tough season with a coach who is "this close" to a championship, you won't teach the right lessons by meeting with the coach to complain about your kid's playing time. Moreover, complaining to a coach about his game-time decisions may just make your child's difficult situation even worse.

Also, never forget: we're preparing "the child for the path, not the path for the child."

In this teachable moment, acknowledge to your child that things aren't going as she had hoped, or even as you expected, but there is still something to be gained by continuing to work hard and staying engaged. You could say, "I know you're frustrated because you aren't getting the chance to play as much as you'd like, and I wish things were going differently. But you can contribute to the team in other ways. Work hard at practice, because you are preparing the starters for the game, and cheer and encourage them during games so they know you're supporting them. Coaches notice and appreciate hard work and a positive attitude."

In elementary school, my kids weren't typically in the starting line-up, and often didn't play when the outcome of the game was on the line. But they generally enjoyed their experiences, because we encouraged them to always go for the "most improved" award at the end of the season. That's the distinction that proves you always gave the team your best effort. (They didn't always win that award, by the way. Not the point!)

During their years of instructional sports, children are taught that the most important values in sports are equal participation and equal recognition. But as they get older and the emphasis on competition increases, they're confronted with the cold, hard fact that life isn't always fair. Not everyone has the same talents, not everyone gets the same playing time, and not everyone will have the same experience as part of the team. But having a positive attitude and doing your best engenders purpose and pride, and ultimately, that's what makes someone a valuable teammate.

I have always tried to be true to myself,
to pick those battles I felt were important.
My ultimate responsibility is to myself.
I could never be anything else.

—ARTHUR ASHE

8. The moment: Your state's high school athletic association has adopted broad new recommendations about inclusion for transgendered student-athletes. Their policy promotes the practice of allowing such students to play on sports teams and use facilities based on the gender with which they identify, not based on their biological sex. They further recommend that all student-athletes should be taught about acceptance of transgendered persons to avoid potential discrimination.

As a Christian, you believe every individual should be treated with dignity and respect, but you have profound concerns about the growing trend to normalize transgenderism, rather than consider it a serious medical or psychological condition. The political correctness that permeates public school policies undoubtedly will prevail on this issue. What will you teach your child about this delicate and confusing subject?

As we know, America's public schools are petri dishes for social engineering, and no issue has become more prevalent in curriculum, health, or school safety than LGBTQ acceptance. The subject of transgenderism is driving significant policy changes at every governmental level, and these standards will directly impact sports programs for children. It's likely that our kids will encounter transgenderism—at least hypothetically through training and policy requirements—at some point during their school years.

As stated in chapter 3, the Los Angeles County Department of Public Health reports that the incidence of transgenderism among our population remains infinitesimally small, and is exceedingly rare among children. Yet recent media attention on individuals, especially children, who seek medical treatment for a gender identity disorder has brought the issue to the forefront. The stories of these kids are heart-wrenching. Anyone would feel sympathy based on the portrayals on television. Who couldn't have compassion for a child who feels out of place in his or her own body?

Many Christians aren't even sure what our faith teaches about this subject. It's important to understand that there is a medical condition known as gender-identity disorder, which is biological in nature, which the Catholic Church, at least, recognizes as a legitimate disorder. But other kinds of transsexual or transgender behaviors have historically been considered mental or emotional, and in adults, they are overwhelmingly sexual in nature. In the past, the solution was not to adapt the body to the disorder, but to treat the deep psychological issues at the root of the problem. As Christians, we hold fast to the belief that God, the Creator of the universe and of each person in it, determines our gender by our sex and wants us to honor and protect our bodies as he created them. That's in direct conflict with the emerging idea that gender is a social construct, and that individuals are free to define (and even redefine) their gender based on their feelings.

This topic is so confusing to children that I believe it should be avoided, at least until kids reach middle school. Unfortunately, depending on what area of the country you live in, the school system may force you to discuss it with children as young as kindergarten or first grade, since it may come up in other contexts. Assuming you're able to avoid the subject of transgenderism until your child reaches adolescence, you could broach the subject with questions such as, "I'm wondering if you've ever heard the word *transgender*, or if you know what it means?" Gauging what your child already knows is a good starting point.

If your state or school district adopts a transgendered athlete policy, you could discuss it with your child by saying, "Honestly, I don't understand what goes on in the hearts and minds of people who feel they are the wrong gender, but I believe they need our prayers so that they can learn to love and respect the bodies and the identities that God created for them. Even if we have questions about transgenderism or we might disagree with someone's decision to get medical treatment that changes their bodies, we never treat people differently or unkindly just because we don't understand them. Being around a transgendered person might make you uncomfortable, but God challenges us to love everyone, even (especially!) people who make us uncomfortable."

Policies meant to protect transgendered kids can have the opposite impact on the rest of the students, causing others to feel awkward about sharing facilities or playing with or against someone who is transgendered. If you encounter such a situation, you should advocate for your child and express your concerns to the appropriate people. Far too often in this culture, Christian parents are made to feel guilty or accused of bigotry simply because they speak out for their kids and their values. But even in our politically correct world, you have the right and the obligation to protect your child.

No matter how you respond to your school, the lessons for your child's character and evolving understanding of faith are crucial. If you encounter a situation like this, repeat this message frequently: "God calls us to honor the dignity of each person, even if we believe they are following the wrong path. Being kind doesn't mean you agree with what someone is doing, it just means we're presenting the face of Jesus to a person who needs his love. Other than treating people with kindness, God wants our prayers for a child who struggles with his or her identity. That's the most effective way we can help."

> **Treat a person as he is,**
> **and he will remain as he is.**
> **Treat him as he could become,**
> **and he will become what he should be.**
>
> **—JIMMY JOHNSON**

9. The moment: Your child's youth soccer coach allows parents to stay for the team's 90-minute practices two afternoons a week. At most practices, at least one parent of each child does so. More than that, they often cheer and encourage their kids the same way they do at regular games, and even take photos and videos of the practices. Not only do you think this is a waste of your time, you also believe it's not in your child's best interest to have you hover over his activities like a groupie at a Hollywood premiere. How does helicopter parenting help your child to become independent, responsible, self-reliant, and resourceful?

Rhetorical question alert! By now, you can probably guess what I'm going to say: Helicopter parenting is all about the parents. If you want to raise independent kids, you have to drive away from your kid's activities and trust that they'll be just fine without you.

You'd think that coaches would discourage parents from attending practices (and by *discourage* I mean "ban them entirely") so children could focus on learning drills and plays, and not on their parents' glowing approval, or lack of it. The idea that Mom and Dad would drop everything on a weekday to sit in the stands with a camcorder sounds more like a *Saturday Night Live* skit than real life, but it's a new norm for parental involvement. The Liberty Mutual Insurance Responsible Sports survey revealed that nine out of ten parents claim they are involved in their kids' sports by attending practices or games.

Interestingly, nearly half of the coaches polled—46 percent—said *lack* of parental involvement was a problem. Once again, parents and coaches aren't on the same page. Perhaps the reason coaches don't perceive parental involvement is that they're not interested in the folks who show up to take pictures of their kids practicing their sport. They want adults in sneakers, helping to execute drills and keep kids constructively occupied.

The larger parenting question is about helping kids to learn independence, self-confidence, self-reliance, and resourcefulness—traits and skills that can only be gained through experience. Hovering over children eliminates the avenues to internalizing these character traits and, worse, can cause kids to feel anxious and afraid because they surmise, correctly, that you don't believe they'll be safe without them.

Hovering isn't exclusive to sports. From Scout meetings to cherub choir, private music lessons to advanced math classes, it's typical to find parents sitting in a corner, reading a book or scrolling on a tablet, but invariably listening closely to the direction and instruction of the adults they are paying to spend time with their kids. It's important to be appropriately involved in our kids' stuff, and coaches and instructors are happy to find ways to let you help them. But serving as a permanent cheering section for your child isn't involvement; it's an excess of attention that feeds the narcissistic self-absorption for which our kids' generation is becoming known.

Children are hard-wired for independence. From the time they're toddlers, they resist parental intervention with a confident, "All by myself!" Perhaps the only way to ground the parental helicopter is to make the conscious decision not to buy into the myth that our kids need us in every moment. Then, instead of driving home from a practice or lesson reviewing what you just saw and heard, your child will take ownership of his own activity by telling you about what he did and learned.

> Whatever you do in life,
> surround yourself with smart people
> who'll argue with you.
> —JOHN WOODEN

10. The moment: Your husband volunteers to coach your child's soccer team, an idea you supported wholeheartedly. It would give your husband a chance to be more involved in your son's activities, and allow the two of them to spend time together. Your husband played soccer in high school and college, so he knows the sport inside and out. He's also a great teacher, and the kids respond well to his caring and supportive coaching style. However, your son isn't the most talented player on the team, and you sense tension growing between them because your husband has high expectations for your son's athletic abilities. What should be a positive shared activity sometimes turns into a stressful, emotional roller coaster as father and son spar about soccer. How can you use this sticky situation to help your child grow in character and maturity? (Not to mention, how can you defuse the tension at your dinner table?)

Okay, you caught me. This was us, but it wasn't soccer; it was basketball. My husband, Jim, is a longtime—and awesome—basketball coach who has coached hundreds of kids, from peewees to high schoolers. His lifelong love of the game and exceptional teaching skills have created wonderful athletic experiences for countless kids, no matter their abilities. I'm sure this sounds like I'm bragging, but it's true. (And if I were bragging, I would have mentioned that he could still dunk a basketball until he was forty-eight years old, something he did every year on his birthday until they "raised the official height of the hoops." So clearly I'm not.)

This situation presents some advantages for the "coach's kid," as well as a few inherent difficulties. Your child is likely to get some extra instruction in the driveway from an adult who is personally invested in his success. While the rest of the team has to share the attention of the coach at practice, your child gets the team's leader all to himself on the ride home to evaluate his game, discuss his on-court decision-making, and learn how to excel.

But that undivided attention and personal instruction is also the downside. The rest of the kids get to climb into the car, report that "practice was fine," and head home for dinner, homework, and a shower. The coach's kid might enjoy a night of that sort of normalcy, but the conversation on his ride home is likely to be much more technical, and there's a good chance he'll feel like he's sitting under a microscope through which his dad will now dissect all of his efforts.

According to my husband, coaches are typically harder on their own kids, partly because they have to establish credibility with the rest of the team. If the other kids perceive that the coach's child gets special treatment or isn't held to the same standard as everyone else, both the coach and his child lose the respect of the team.

This scenario is made all the more likely by the fact that 85 percent of youth sports coaches are dads coaching their own kids. Obviously, youth sports programs would not exist without parental participation, and it's an especially excellent way for men to be involved in the lives of their children, but it also means there will be conflicts because of the role a father might play on his child's sports team. Not only is there the possibility of conflict between dads and their children but also things can get sticky when issues arise with other kids on the team, or with their parents. If you're a parent considering volunteering to coach your child's team, be forewarned: conflict is an occupational hazard.

Overall, the experience was positive for both Jim and Jimmy, even if there were occasional sparks between them. By the time Jimmy got to be an eighth grader, he had a better understanding of the game than most of the guys on his team. But he wasn't the best player, in part because he was younger and less developed than some of his teammates, and also because at that time, his mental aptitude for the game exceeded his abilities. It was not uncommon for my two guys to come into the house bickering about something that had happened at practice, and these conversations got heated because they often straddled the fence between their relationships as father and son, coach and player.

Most of the time, I tried to counsel them individually about how to communicate more effectively. I'd say to Jim, "You have to be careful not to make Jimmy feel that you're pressuring him to be better. He's doing his best. He should have the same enthusiasm from his dad that the other guys get from their fathers." And to Jimmy I would say, "You're lucky to have a dad who is such a great teacher of the game. Take advantage of that and don't get defensive. He's not criticizing you. He's instructing, just like he would do with the other guys. They don't take his comments personally, and neither should you."

A few times, I called a summit in the den to remind my men that the whole reason they were playing basketball together was to enjoy one another and have fun with a sport they both loved. In those conversations, I tried to elevate the discussion from the nitpicky issues they were focused on and get them to see the bigger picture of how to communicate more effectively as father and son. Fortunately, they were incredibly close, so it didn't take them long to get "unstuck." But even parents and children who aren't particularly close can benefit and enjoy a stronger relationship if they use their shared struggles on and off the court to promote better and more open communication.

No matter how difficult it might be from time to time, the participation of parents as coaches and organizers of kids' activities is a crucial way for children to experience the love and leadership of their dads and moms. When things get tense, it's best to recognize the unique relationship that exists between a child and his parent/coach and keep the lines of communication open. The priority must be the child's positive experience in the sport, and building an even stronger bond between parent and child. If coaching your own kid doesn't do that, don't raise your hand to volunteer next season.

Instead, get back in the stands and do what your kid needs most—be a loving and supportive parent.

The Lesson Plan

Sports offer a uniquely effective means to teach important life lessons that build solid character and moral strength. The first and most crucial way in which you can use sports to teach good character traits is to exemplify them while supporting your child's athletic pursuits. Your child won't learn to respect his or her coaches, teammates, and opponents if you're griping about the coach's incompetence, your kid's inadequate playing time, or the other team's unfair advantage!

Here are a few other ways to use sports and other extracurricular activities for teachable moments about character, conscience, and faith:

- *Keep your focus on your child's effort and improvement.* Your kid can't control the score or outcome of a game or match, or even whether he or she always has the chance to play. Your child *can* control his or her effort in practices and games, and make measurable improvement over the course of a season. Those things will foster greater self-confidence and enjoyment of the sport.

- *Be your child's emotional support system.* Experts say you can fill a child's "emotional tank" with a mix of five specific, genuine comments of praise for every one criticism or critique. Kids can't be fooled with empty compliments, so don't exaggerate or say things that are obviously untrue. They also don't get much out of vague comments like, "Good game." Find precise reasons to compliment your child's performance, and make your critique equally exact so it's something your child can act on in the future.

- *Put honor first.* Assure that your child understands the things that matter to you the most: Playing fairly, by the rules; treating coaches, teammates, officials, and opponents with respect; exhibiting excellent sportsmanship, win or lose; and keeping the focus on learning and fun.

- *Develop the "Intangibles."* Use sports and other activities to exercise aspects of character and faith: Persevering through adversity, accepting a challenge, tapping into unknown resources of strength and grace, and weaving faith into everyday encounters.

Sharing in our children's athletic and extracurricular pursuits by supporting and encouraging them can be one of the most fun ways in which we teach the life lessons we want to instill. Keep your eye on the ball—your son or daughter's strong heart and good character—and watch your child become a winner in life!

CHAPTER SEVEN

Teachable Moments in the Real World

PERHAPS THE MOST STUNNING discovery you make as a parent is how quickly your children grow up. One day, you're wiping apple sauce from the crevices of pudgy fingers, and the next you're nervously placing your car keys into that same hand with an admonition to drive carefully and get home on time. The years in between pass in a blur of birthday parties, teacher conferences, camping trips, and Christmas mornings. When you're in the middle of it, you hardly have time to notice you're exhausted.

As a friend once said, the days may drag on, but the years fly by.

As we've seen, when children are young, their teachable moments often come from encounters with media and culture that give you the chance to instill your values. When they're older, the most crucial teachable moments come from their personal experiences of freedom and responsibility that put their character to the test. Kids can't demonstrate that they have internalized a moral code or developed a mature conscience unless they have opportunities to make good decisions. But of course, whenever there's a good decision to be made, there's an equally big mistake looming around the corner.

Before you have the chance to forget all the words to the *Sesame Street* theme song, you'll graduate from relatively easy and expected parenting trials to more serious concerns, some of which could have lifelong consequences. As my parents warned me long ago: "Little children, little problems; big children, big problems." Those "big problems" may test your patience and induce insomnia, but they'll also represent some of the most compelling and effective (and sometimes expensive) parenting opportunities that will come your way.

Our Grow-Up-Too-Fast World

Consider this weird phenomenon: In our culture, children are unfazed by extreme violence and sexual themes in their entertainment content; they become precociously involved in dating and romantic relationships because pairing up in early adolescence is typical; they're fully engaged in social media with people their parents may or may not know; they carry their own credit cards and cell phones; they're even allowed to seek medical care for "reproductive health services" without parental consent. And yet, countless communities across the country no longer allow kids to ride their bikes to school. It's too dangerous.

Moreover, municipalities are criminalizing formerly commonplace activities of children's daily lives. Parents who allow their kids to do seemingly safe and appropriate things such as play in a neighborhood park, walk to a nearby store, or ride a bus or subway without an adult present are being arrested and prosecuted. I wish I were exaggerating. Unfortunately, the paranoia that prompts schools to ban games like tag and dodge ball also is inciting the prosecution of parents who let their children roam the earth without a protective layer of bubble wrap.

Our society's obsessive anxiety about child abduction, abuse, and injury—escalated by tabloid journalism—has created a new equation in which worrying equals parental love. It's an environment that makes it almost impossible for children to take risks, conquer their fears, and prove that they're capable of using sound judgment, solving their problems, and protecting themselves in potentially compromising circumstances. In the ultimate cultural irony, kids are sheltered from the *real* world but allowed to be virtually integrated into pop culture, which can do far more damage to their hearts and souls than riding a city bus to the mall.

Molding and Revealing Personal Character

My parenting hero on the issue of promoting freedom and responsibility for our children is my friend, author and columnist Lenore Skenazy, a.k.a. "World's Worst Mom." (Not a joke. Google "World's Worst Mom." She even had a TV show!)

Lenore wrote a column in 2008 for the now-defunct *New York Sun* entitled, "Why I Let My 9-Year-Old Son Ride the Subway Alone," in which she recounted her son's first solo trip on New York's public transportation system. He had been begging her to leave him someplace in the city and let him make his way home. Finally, she agreed and said good-bye in the handbag department of Bloomingdale's. She gave him a subway card, a $20 bill, some quarters, and a map. In under an hour, he walked in the front door of their apartment feeling proud and confident.

Her column caused a national ruckus. Lenore and her son landed on the set of the *Today Show*, where she defended her parental judgment and fielded questions about the possible consequences she had clearly not considered. In actuality, she *had* considered them. That's why she knew that practically all of the "risks" that people most fear are less likely to occur than being hit by lightning . . . in the subway station.

The experience demonstrated to Lenore the crippling fear that now informs parental caution. She has documented, through a terrific book, *Free-Range Kids: How to Raise Safe, Self-Reliant Children (Without Going Nuts with Worry)*, and a website of the same name (freerangekids.com), the insane lengths to which parents now go to safeguard their children, as well as the unintended consequence to our nation's kids of hyper-protective parenting—insecurity, frustration, fear, and an over-reliance on their parents to handle their problems.

When I tell Lenore's story and applaud her smart and brave parenting, even I am labeled lackadaisical. I am negligent by association! But Lenore was hardly lax, and like her, I believe children deserve the chance to build skills and self-confidence by encountering the real world. That's where their character is both molded and revealed.

Now, this doesn't mean I permit every sort of independent activity. For example, I'm not likely to allow my sixteen-year-old daughter to go with a friend, unaccompanied by an adult, to a rock concert at a theatre in the middle of downtown Detroit. (I said no to this scheme, and Amy is still annoyed with me. It's all she wanted for her birthday.) But for her fourteenth birthday, we gave Amy an airline ticket to travel on her own to Washington, DC, to visit her older sister. It was a nonstop flight, she knew how to read airport signage, she had a cell phone and some cash; we figured she'd be fine. In fact, she was more than fine; she was empowered.

What if something had gone wrong? Well, it didn't; but if something had happened that put my daughter in danger or caused her to be injured, I'm certain others would have helped her, and she would have been capable of rising to the occasion to take care of herself. Believing this, and, more importantly, knowing we believed this about her, gave Amy all the strength and courage she needed to do something exciting and fun. Her horizons were broadened and possibilities expanded thanks to the maturity she gained on that trip.

The Lesson Is Larger than the Moment

What about when a teachable moment is the result of a child's bad decision? Let's face it: Sometimes if it weren't for bad decisions, there'd be no decisions at all. They keep us parents in business!

When your kids make poor behavioral choices, you're likely to get wrapped up in the outcome. But you must be careful not to make your anger or frustration the central consequence when kids mess up. If the only takeaway a teen gets from an episode of lying, or shoplifting, or underage drinking or smoking is simply to avoid your wrath by not getting caught, the event won't help them to grow in goodness or faith. The mistakes might be big, but they're never as important as the lessons they can teach.

Now, bad decisions and disobedience must be met with consequences—even punishment—so you can assure that your kids understand how their actions can and do hurt others, as well as themselves. The trick is to deal with the event swiftly so you can focus on the bigger picture, because what's important is not learning that fenders dent when they strike a tree, for example, but that carelessness is a way of acting irresponsibly.

Instead, elevate their misdeeds to the level of significance that lets them know you are using their mistakes for a larger purpose. As we're told in Romans 8:28, "God causes all things to work together for good to those who love the Lord, to those who are called according to His purpose." Everything that kids do wrong is useful if it instructs them, builds their character, and develops a mature conscience.

Finally, don't forget to use your kids' good decisions as teaching tools, too. Whenever they act with integrity, make a sacrifice for the sake of upholding what's right, or demonstrate maturity in a challenging situation, let them know how much you admire them! Offer a "truth bonus"—that is, be sure to reward their honesty when owning up to their mistakes—and let truth-telling mitigate the consequences they might otherwise receive for a poor choice. (For example, if your punishment would typically be erasing all social plans for a couple of weeks, you might allow a single event on a weekend to begin the process of rebuilding trust.) When they accept responsibility and make themselves accountable for their actions, show compassion and trust that they'll get it right the next time.

Our culture makes it easy to take the wrong path. When kids wander from what's right, your ready forgiveness will demonstrate the unconditional love that most closely resembles God's love for us all.

Ten Real-World Teachable Moments

> **If you want children
> to keep their feet on the ground,
> put some responsibility on their shoulders.**
> —PAULINE PHILLIPS (A.K.A. DEAR ABBY)

1. The moment: You have confidence that your ten-year-old is capable of staying at home alone for a few hours at a time. She also is mature enough to supervise her two younger siblings for short periods while you go to the grocery store or run errands. You recall doing the same when you were her age, so this seems appropriate. But when you mention that your daughter is babysitting at home to a friend, she is aghast that you left "a small child" in charge and accuses you of imprudent parenting. Her blunt comments cause you to question your judgment—you thought you were helping your daughter to grow in maturity and responsibility; now you're not so sure.

There's no "right" age to give children added responsibility. Some are mature enough at age nine or ten to walk the dog in the neighborhood, or stay at home alone for an hour at a time, or make macaroni and cheese on the stove. Others aren't ready for those tasks until twelve or thirteen, or older. Most states don't have laws that specify an age when kids can stay home alone, but leave it up to parents. The few states that have set an age prove there's no agreement on this question. In Illinois, kids must be fourteen; in Maryland, they must be at least eight; in Oregon, it's ten.

I think moms and dads know when their kids are ready to stay home alone for brief periods of time. You recognize a child who can take care of her physical needs, who knows what to do in an emergency, who generally makes good decisions, and who isn't afraid to be alone. There's no guarantee that everything will go perfectly when you leave your ten- or eleven-year-old by herself, but chances are she's paying closer attention than a sixteen-year-old might! Your confidence in your child is the most important factor in this decision.

Children aren't much different today than they were in the days of American pioneers, when they were capable of following the wagon train and even helping to kill and cook an opossum or two along the way. Today, we don't let kids use a microwave without adult supervision. How did they get to be so inept?

The answer is: it's not them; it's us.

Just think twice before you mention to a friend that your tween is home alone! The media and our fearful parenting culture have convinced folks that children are inherently at risk if there isn't an adult within arm's reach, which is why hovering now defines "responsible parenting." If you admit that you don't monitor your child's every move, your friends may label you negligent, or at least careless. Though many parents won't share your belief that kids need experiences of freedom and responsibility, the fruits of this parenting strategy will be evident when yours are the most trustworthy and self-reliant teens you know.

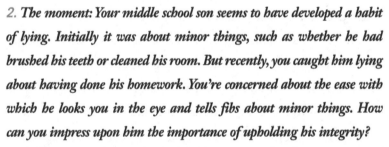

> Well, when I was younger,
> I lied all the time,
> because once you understand
> the power of lying, it's really like magic,
> because you transform reality for people.
>
> —LOUIS C. K.

*2. **The moment:** Your middle school son seems to have developed a habit of lying. Initially it was about minor things, such as whether he had brushed his teeth or cleaned his room. But recently, you caught him lying about having done his homework. You're concerned about the ease with which he looks you in the eye and tells fibs about minor things. How can you impress upon him the importance of upholding his integrity?*

I'll never understand why children try to lie their way out of things. They're terrible liars. Case in point: I once asked my son if he put the dog out to do his morning business. My son said "yes," so it seemed odd that the dog was scratching at the back door. I opened the door to offer the pup a second chance, thinking maybe his little canine kidneys were working overtime, only to discover fresh, white snow covering the back steps. No dog tracks, no yellow evidence of doggy relief, only the obvious proof my son lied to my face.

Child development experts reassure us that lying comes at age-appropriate intervals. A 2010 study from researchers at Toronto

University says lying is evidence that kids are developing intelligence. In a study with 1,200 children aged two to seventeen, researchers determined that only 20 percent of two-year-olds were capable of lying, while 90 percent of four-year-olds could. Lying skills peak at about age twelve.

Or whenever you shout from the kitchen: "Who left the dirty dishes in the sink?" And all of your kids reply, "Not me!"

Lying is, in fact, normal developmental behavior. First, kids lie to get what they want. Later, they lie to stay out of trouble. Supposedly, they grow out of it. But here's my problem with this theory: Some people don't grow out of it. As children, they lie to their teachers to avoid detention. Later, they lie to a grand jury to avoid incarceration. These people are called "liars," and they're everywhere.

Plus, I believe a nine-year-old who lies about something minor, like putting his dog out, will absolutely lie at nineteen about where he was until four A.M. and why he smells like a Texas roadhouse. This is why I used to make a fuss about white lies that seemed inconsequential; it wasn't the lie that mattered to me, but the willingness to tell it that told me about the state of my kid's conscience.

And when I say *fuss*, I mean I made a big deal about lying. One episode that put me over the edge involved my son's sloppy attempt to sneak contraband into school—Sharpie permanent markers. When I confronted him, he said he didn't know where they came from. Apparently he expected me to believe they materialized out of thin air and found their way into his backpack.

The way I reacted, you'd have thought he was a regular villain on *Law and Order*. I got a full-blown sermon going, my vocal cords inflamed, veins bulging out of my neck. I told him he was ruining his relationship with me because I couldn't trust him. I told him his deceitful behavior was getting to be a bad habit. I even told him he was a lousy liar anyway, and he lied about things that were just plain stupid. "Dumb and dishonest is no way to go through life," I concluded. Okay, it was a little harsh, but if your mom won't be straight with you, who will?

And anyway, he got over it. I remember he spent a whole day on the dark side of a mother's love. Not even an unsolicited offer to take out the garbage could get a smile out of me. Later that night, he gave me a note. "Dear Mom, I'm writing you this letter to say that I am very sorry that I lied to you . . . I know it's important to be trustworthy." It's signed "your loving son." As though I wouldn't know it was from him.

I remember telling him, "You're going to make a lot of mistakes in life—we all do. Just don't make the mistake of losing your integrity."

The ability to lie may demonstrate that kids are smart, but telling the truth shows they are children of good character. What could be more important?

> It's very important for people
> to know themselves and understand
> what their value system is, because
> if you don't know what your value system is,
> then you don't know what risks are worth
> taking and which ones are worth avoiding.
>
> —DR. BEN CARSON

*3. **The moment: Your teen does something stupid but common for his age—he gets a speeding ticket, or has a car accident, or is caught toilet-papering the house of a fellow student, or is caught at a house party where kids are drinking, or is seen by a neighbor lighting a cigarette in his car—or all of the above. How can you use his acts of bad judgment to your advantage as you build his character and help develop his conscience?***

Every family has its traditions, those rites of passage that demonstrate that a child is maturing into young adulthood, ready to spread his or her wings and make a mark in the wider world. In our family, it's the day you have to call Uncle Tom, a lawyer and retired judge, and ask him to appear with you in district court for your first traffic ticket.

No matter how many times we warn children about the possible consequences of their carelessness, or how often we admonish them to make good choices and be responsible, they're going to mess up. The question isn't "if" or even "how," but rather, "What will they learn when they inevitably make mistakes?"

As parents, our prayers are answered if the worst mistakes our kids make end in a financial penalty, a school suspension, or a minor legal consequence. Anytime a child or teen makes a misstep that results in discipline, rather than a lifetime of pain, suffering, or regret, they're blessed. So it's important we keep things in perspective when kids misbehave. We'd rather they didn't make poor choices, but by forcing children to confront the serious ramifications of their actions, we can help them learn the most compelling and meaningful life lessons.

In other words, take heart. Spray-painting the boys' locker room will not be for naught.

But still . . . spray-painting the locker room? Dining and dashing from Denny's? Climbing a water tower? Running the fast food drive-thru "handoff" play? When you find out about the antics your child pulls, you can't help but ask, "What was he *thinking*?"

Just don't ask *him* what he was thinking because the answer is, he wasn't. Really. It's scientific.

According to the National Institute of Mental Health, research proves that the part of the brain that influences risk-taking and impulsivity doesn't fully develop until the mid-twenties. So at the same time they are enjoying some newfound freedom and mobility, teens and young adults are still generally incapable of accurately assessing and avoiding risk. At last, science has discovered the basis for the time-honored catchall "youthful indiscretion."

Perhaps knowing that physiology plays a role will help some parents accept that their children are capable of colossal acts of misjudgment. Some seem blind to their children's actions, unwilling to imagine that their "good" kids would make grave mistakes. Rather than confront their children's behavior, these parents come to their kid's defense, claiming, "*My* son/daughter would never do XYZ terrible thing."

I hate to break it to you, but so-called troublemakers are not the only ones making trouble. "Good" kids—God-fearing kids who love Jesus, their grandmas, and puppies; kids who play sports and do their homework and the dishes without being asked; kids who belong to youth groups and go on mission trips and volunteer at nursing homes; kids who get jobs and babysit the neighbors and walk dogs— *great* kids—make foolish behavioral choices. It's how they deal with them that exposes the quality of their character.

Of course, the fact that every child is likely to make mistakes doesn't make those poor choices okay. Neither does the fact that parents may have done some equally dopey things when they were teenagers. Yet some parents use both of these facts to justify their kid's experimentation and rebellion.

Many parents chalk up their kids' misdeeds to the culturally accepted idea that misbehaving is to be expected, so there's no point in making a big deal out of it. They even send their children the strong message that the worst thing is getting caught. This is perhaps the most tragic response a parent could give, since it negates any character lesson you might teach in the wake of an episode of poor judgment. The point isn't to minimize the action or brush it aside because it's commonplace, but to use it as a catalyst for growth.

When your child calls with the news that he's been in an accident, or been caught at a party, or been detained by the mall security staff, or (insert your own stressful/expensive detail here), obviously the first thing you must do is deal with the episode at hand. But when the dust settles, you'll need to thoughtfully and prayerfully evaluate what happened and consider what lessons your child can learn from his mistake.

You're likely to be angry and the situation may, indeed, warrant a significant punishment, but my rule of thumb is: The larger the misdeed, the softer your voice must be in response. Teens will expect you to be hopping mad, and you may well be, but your voice should convey the gravity of the situation. Your demeanor must reflect your serious concern.

As you talk about the incident with your child, keep your focus on the elements of character that can best be learned in the midst of a difficult situation: accountability, courage, humility, and forgiveness. You might say, "There's nothing you can do to change the decision you made, but you can show your genuine character by taking responsibility for your actions, accepting the consequences with maturity, and making things right. No matter how bad it seems, you can always recover from your mistakes if you face up to them and you're willing to accept the outcome without complaint and without making excuses for yourself. I'm not happy about your behavior, but I'm proud of you when you own up to it and show that you're willing to learn from it. That's how you demonstrate your character."

Kids need to see that their blunders don't make them less lovable. When you demonstrate love and forgiveness, and support your kids while they rectify their actions, you reveal to them the love that God has for them, even when their behavior is disappointing at best. When they're "shocked" by your love in the midst of their biggest failures, you can teach your children that their mistakes never define them; only their response to the adversities they endure because of them.

It stinks to mess up. But there's no better way to be molded into the person God intends for us to be. Come to think of it, that's probably why he allows us to be so . . . human.

> **Lying is like alcoholism.**
> **You are always recovering.**
> —STEVEN SODERBERGH

4. *The moment: Your high schooler attends a huge house party where the host's parents were supposedly in attendance and supervising.*

When he gets home, he tells you there were no issues with drinking or drugs; it was a clean and fun party. Nothing about his behavior leads you to suspect otherwise. But within a few days, you learn through administrators at his school and other parents that many of the kids in attendance were using drugs and alcohol, the police were called to the home, and the party had turned into a free-for-all. You confront your son, but he's defensive because he says he didn't personally do those things, so he doesn't see why you're upset with him. What should you focus on in the aftermath of such an event?

This is a trick question.

On the one hand, you have every reason to be upset that your son has lied to you and to be angry that he didn't use good judgment and leave a party where others were using alcohol or drugs. You've frequently reminded him that if he's ever in exactly that situation, he should leave or call home for a ride. Moreover, his dishonesty about the nature of the party undermines your trust.

But let's suppose for the sake of argument that you confirm that your son really didn't do anything wrong at the party. He hung out with his friends, who also were not misbehaving, danced, chatted with girls, ate pizza, and comported himself just as you would have hoped. Let's even say he was offered alcohol and turned it down, and also called out his peers for their risky and stupid actions.

Isn't his behavior at the party exactly what you hope he'll do in the future, when he's at college or moves out on his own? And aren't you relieved to know that he acted responsibly, even vocalizing his opinion that his peers' behavior was wrong?

Episodes like this prove that maturing is a process, not an event. As they put a toe in the volatile waters of young adulthood, our kids are

likely to exhibit moments of goodness and moments of . . . well . . . me-
diocrity. Sometimes they even happen at the same time. The tricky
parenting maneuver in circumstances like this is to reinforce the good
stuff while focusing on the character issue that concerns you—in this
case, lying.

We have to give our teens credit for knowing the rules and understanding that their parents will be upset when they break them.
At the risk of overstating the obvious, this is why kids lie. They don't
want to get in trouble.

But suppose you made that deal with your teen that the truth will
always be rewarded—even if the reward is only mitigation of the consequences for whatever misjudgment was made. If you create an atmosphere in which your teenager trusts you not to freak out, he'll be more
likely to tell you the truth about where he goes and what he's doing.

Let's be real: even if you create a policy for a truth bonus, as pro-
posed in chapter 6, your teens still aren't going to tell you everything they're doing when they're out with their friends, because if
they did, they'd have to listen to lectures from you about why it's a
bad idea to drive to Flint just to go to the Sonic drive-through, for
example (winking at you, Betsy Hicks). But they have to know, without doubt or reservation, that they *could* tell you absolutely anything
and you would forgive them.

The way to create that sort of atmosphere is to surprise your
teen with grace. In a situation such as this, you might say, "I'm disappointed that you didn't come home and tell us exactly what went
down at the party. Obviously you knew that we'd be upset that you
didn't leave when you saw that kids were drinking and smoking
weed. But we also know you didn't do those things, and you wanted

to hang out with your friends, and we appreciate that you also set a good example for other kids and spoke up about what you knew was misbehavior. When you get to college or move out on your own, you're often going to find yourself at parties like that, and it's good to know you will make smart decisions about your behavior. But still, as long as you're in high school, we have to insist that you follow our rules about parties—if there's alcohol or drugs, you absolutely have to leave. And in the future, if you want us to trust you, you have to trust *us* by telling us the truth."

Then, instead of levying a punishment, prove your point. Just talk about the party. Ask questions about who was there and who your child hung out with. Ask what kind of behavior he witnessed, but also whether there was good food and if anyone danced or played cards. Don't interrogate him—just talk! Talk, without judging, without disapproving, without lecturing. Show him what it would look like to open up and let you peek behind his veil of teenage secrecy. If you use that conversation to affirm his behavior and demonstrate your support, you'll establish a new level of expectations that assume greater maturity on his part, and therefore, greater accountability.

Keep in mind that the role of parent never ends, but it must change as your children get older. As you guide them toward a more adult way of communicating with you, you'll find new ways to instill your values and lead your children toward maturity.

> **Just because you can afford it doesn't mean you should buy it.**
> —SUZE ORMAN

5. The moment: Your teens have their own money from babysitting, part-time jobs, and birthday gifts. They want to buy things that you don't approve of, such as certain clothes and video games. They don't think their decisions should be subject to your approval since they are spending their own money. How much control should you assert over your kids' spending choices when you aren't providing the funds?

Who doesn't love the feeling when your child asks for permission to go to a movie with his pals, but doesn't ask for money? In addition to offering opportunities to become more responsible and experience some independence, having their own money means your kids won't need yours. Of course, it's a false sense of liberation, because . . . well . . . college. But still.

Experts suggest teaching children about money from their earliest years and establishing good habits by dividing all income (money from birthdays, babysitting, allowance, chores, part-time jobs) into four separate "banks" marked "give," "grow," "save," and "spend." Money from the "give" bank is earmarked for church and the charities of your child's choice. The "grow" fund is like a retirement account (you might even match funds deposited to it, in the same way an employer would). The "save" fund is meant for larger purchases or special events such as a school trip—things that require a bigger chunk of accumulated cash—and the "spend" bank is meant for regular purchases and socializing. (You can certainly open multiple accounts in an actual financial institution, but you don't have to, especially at first.)

When it comes to spending their own money, mere ownership of the funds doesn't entitle children to total control over their spending decisions. You're still the parent, regardless of whether your children have their own money, and your role as the parent—the one who knows what is best for your kids—trumps any financial freedom your children might believe they enjoy. So, just because your son has the funds for an Xbox 360, or a pet snake, or a hardly rusty F-150 pickup does not mean he can make the choice to buy those things. Similarly, your daughter should not feel free to buy and wear make-up, or purchase clothing that you object to, or have extensions or color added to her hair just because she can pay for it.

When it comes to money, it's critical to teach children that the use of financial resources is a value-laden choice. Oddly, this is a lesson many parents don't model. For example, I know a mom who once complained to me that she loathed everything about the Victoria's Secret PINK store. She felt the clothing was too sexy and skimpy for her tween and teen girls, and that their advertising and store displays exploited girls and women. She didn't like the image the product line projected, and she especially disliked the trademarked "PINK" across the backside of all of the shorts and sweats, meant to draw attention to girls' rear ends. "But my two daughters love the stuff and that's what they want to wear," she told me, "So we have closets full of PINK clothing. It just bugs me every time I have to pull out a credit card and buy that stuff."

I was dumbfounded by the lack of consistency between that woman's stated values about immodest clothing and the exploitation of women and girls, and her behavior—shelling out money she didn't want to spend on items she believed were affirmatively bad for her daughters. (I didn't want to say that to her face, of course, so I wrote a newspaper column about it instead. Moral of the story: be careful what you say in front of me.) How are we to teach our children to spend their money in ways that support and demonstrate their values if we're doing exactly the opposite—especially if we're buying things for *them* that we don't want them to own?

That was rhetorical, obviously. The answer is, you can't.

The first guideline about spending, then, is to model the behavior you want your kids to emulate. Make sure your purchases reflect your values, and say no to those that don't. Whether you are concerned about cost, content, ethical production, modesty, age-appropriateness, or any other factor that might give you pause, be sure to explain to your children why you won't use your money in a particular way so that they make the connection between values and spending.

A second rule about spending is: parental approval required. You might establish parameters within which your kids can make some choices, but as a general rule, even when they're spending their own funds, you should expect that they check to be sure that their selections are okay with you. This is especially true for media purchases, which can seem appropriate, but often may contain content to which you object.

Finally, in our materialistic culture, parents are challenged to demonstrate to our kids that having more stuff is not the route to happiness or popularity. This is perhaps the most crucial reason to maintain control over spending: to keep children from the habit of buying their way into social circles, or deluding themselves into thinking that they will be more content if they have the latest version of everything. It's not an easy lesson to convey, but it's crucial if our kids are to avoid the empty pursuit of consumerism.

Whenever the subject of "stuff" arises, be sure to reiterate the irrefutable principle that money doesn't buy happiness, and that the path to real contentment is to need and want *less*. Focus instead on the cool person your child is becoming—not because she owns cool things, but because she defines herself by her character.

> When your mother asks, "Do you want a piece of advice?" it is a mere formality. It doesn't matter if you answer yes or no. You're going to get it anyway.
>
> —ERMA BOMBECK

6. The moment: You press "play" on the CD player in your car and find yourself listening to an album your son left in the player, a compilation of current rap music. You're stunned by the language in the songs. The profanity isn't as troubling as the racial epithets and references to drugs, violence, misogyny, and racial hatred. You hadn't realized your son was listening to such graphic and offensive music. What should you focus on when you discuss this with him, or should you respect his right to listen to his choice of music?

Yep, this happened. While driving to a speaking engagement in northern Michigan, I pressed a button on my car stereo and discovered that my college-aged son had left a rap compilation album in the CD rotation. It included cuts from Jay Z's *Magna Carta Holy Grail* and Kanye West's *Yeezus*.

I was horrified.

Now, I'm not a prude. I have four children between the ages of sixteen and twenty-four. I'm known for the occasional salty turn of phrase, and I make my living as a culture commentator whose specialty is informing other parents about the things their kids are consuming in the media. I'm about as tuned in as a fiftysomething woman can be without dressing like a teenager. But listening to Jay Z and Kanye West revealed to me how desensitized our children's generation has become to content that ought to be offensive to everyone. I'm not even talking about the constant use of the "f-word," the misogyny, the glorification of drugs and violence, the anti-authoritarianism, the pornographic descriptions of sex, or even the worship of money, all of which make this music abhorrent at best. Nope, the thing that caused a visceral response for me, that prevented me from listening to even one song all the way through just to inform myself of what was on the album, was the constant use of the "n-word" in the lyrics.

My husband and I grew up in homes where that word was never uttered or permitted, not out of political correctness, but because of the racism it reflects. It's alarming to me that the mere sound of that word wouldn't prompt someone to gasp and change the song as if the car stereo were about to explode. Instead, people growing up in our children's generation sing along—disappointingly, my kids included.

On the way home from that speaking trip, I thought and prayed about how to approach this issue. I realized that if my young adult children were not offended by the lyrics in some of their music, at least they should know that I am deeply insulted by them. What ensued was a compelling series of conversations that covered a broad range of issues: race, respect, pop culture, hypocrisy, Miley Cyrus's faux "hood" behavior, Kanye and Jay Z's "messiah complexes," twenty-first-century poetry, socioeconomic "posing," and more.

I learned a lot about the ways in which our children's generation has been shaped by rap, hip-hop, and pop music. My daughter Betsy, a college grad with a degree in mass communications and an affinity for every kind of music, argued that the concept of "in-speak" applies in rap, that is, the idea that people from a certain group may use otherwise offensive words or phrases among themselves, but others may not use them. Thus, black people can use racial epithets that white people can't, and gays can use slurs among themselves that heterosexuals may not use. If you're outside a particular group, apparently you omit those words when you're singing along, a solution that feels like relativism set to "mad beats."

I made it clear to my kids that I don't object to any particular style of music; I actually like the sound of rap sometimes, especially Christian rap, and some hip-hop music evokes my Motown childhood. I also know that every generation has its own sound, and that music is a powerful tool for teens and young adults to express themselves. But I challenged them to consider whether they are desensitized to material that they would never permit to be spoken in their presence, and further, whether listening to and supporting certain artists makes them partly responsible for our cultural debasement.

In the end, I decided to declare that some lyrics may not be played under my roof or on any device that I purchase or provide. I explained, "I'm sorry if this makes you angry or annoyed at me. I'm not trying to police your music choices, I'm trying to be morally consistent, and for me, it is absurd to say that I believe what I believe but then to allow words and phrases that wound my spirit to be played in my home or car."

These days, understanding how our kids engage with pop culture and monitoring the content of their media diets have become major parental responsibilities. When they're young, children need your direct instruction about music and entertainment choices so that you can explain and instill your values. But there's still a role to play when they get old enough to choose for themselves: Setting an example and living authentically according to Gospel values so that grown children can see firsthand what it looks like to apply those values to their daily lives.

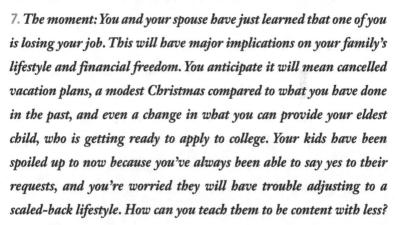

Hitting bottom and hitting it hard was the worst thing that ever happened to me and the best thing that ever happened to me.
—DAVE RAMSEY

7. The moment: You and your spouse have just learned that one of you is losing your job. This will have major implications on your family's lifestyle and financial freedom. You anticipate it will mean cancelled vacation plans, a modest Christmas compared to what you have done in the past, and even a change in what you can provide your eldest child, who is getting ready to apply to college. Your kids have been spoiled up to now because you've always been able to say yes to their requests, and you're worried they will have trouble adjusting to a scaled-back lifestyle. How can you teach them to be content with less?

Hundreds of thousands of families have experienced or will experience the impact of unemployment and economic reversals. In fact, some financial gurus say it's not *if* you'll hit hard times, but *when*, because everyone goes through some sort of financial difficulty at some point. When that time comes, parents can be poised to instill some of the most crucial, life-changing lessons they'll ever teach. One of those lessons is the exhilarating freedom of the word "no."

In 2008, after the housing bubble burst and the markets caved, I wrote a column in which I argued that the financial crisis might have been the best thing that could have happened to American parenting in our lifetimes, because at long last, moms and dads were forced to say no to their children. This notion was so unheard of that I landed on the *CBS Evening News*, explaining to a reporter exactly how parents would do that.

"Do what?" I said.

"Say 'no,'" the reporter clarified.

"Well, at our house, we do it like this: 'No.'"

He nodded, like reporters do. I'm not kidding.

Our consumer culture has created attitudes of materialism in our children. American parents have not resisted this development but rather have fed it like a hungry beast. Even when we don't have adequate financial resources to give our kids the things they ask for, we stretch ourselves thin so that they have the latest gadgets, games, fashions, and fads. This might be due to cultural conditioning on the part of advertisers and marketers, or it could be we're a generation of parents that is so insecure about our kids' affection that we regularly reaffirm it with gifts, just to feel loved. Or maybe it's just easier to give kids new things than it is to listen to them beg.

Regardless, our children are accustomed to having pretty much everything they want and a lot of stuff they don't need.

Moreover, according to a study from the American Institute of CPAs (AICPA), American children are also accustomed to receiving an average of $65 per month in allowance, more or less, depending on their ages. A majority of kids also get paid for good grades. Clearly, a financial reversal for the adults in the home will have an impact on the day-to-day lifestyles of children who are used to regular infusions of cash and the freedom that it buys.

An economic downturn will require the family to sacrifice together. It's a bad idea to bear the burden of a job loss or financial hardship in a way that lets your children believe they are immune to its effects. While you might want to protect your children from the impact of financial struggles, doing so teaches the lesson, "Spoiling you is more important than living responsibly as a family." It also eliminates the opportunity for children to learn that contentment in life is free.

But if you never say no, it's hard to say no. Also, if you've used stuff to get your kids to cooperate with your requests, or if you generally offer to buy things or give money to motivate a child's ambition, you may discover that your child's values are more centered on money and stuff than you have appreciated.

How much you tell your children about your financial picture depends on their ages. It's important to share information with kids without sharing your stress or anxiety. They count on adults to know what to do, not burden them with adult worries and fears. Little children need only be told, "Mom and Dad are working hard to be responsible, and that means saving money and making do with what we have. So from now on, we're going to buy less stuff and think more carefully about the way we choose to spend our money."

Older kids and teens ought to be made aware of any employment or income changes in a way that enables them to exhibit understanding, compassion, and responsibility as members of the family. You might say, "Things will be tight for us until we are able to find a way to replace our income, but we want you to know that we're confident that we'll get through this situation. We're counting on you to accept that things may seem difficult. You won't always be able to do the things you're used to doing. We're going to have to cut back in order to make ends meet, but this situation is a great reminder that our financial circumstances don't define our happiness."

It's frustrating to have to deny kids things because you can't afford them, but even if you have the resources to give your children the things they want, it's a good idea to say no frequently. Children can't learn to defer gratification or deny their impulses if every wish is granted.

Focus instead on gratitude and teach children to be thankful to God for what they *do* have: a loving family, caring friends, and Christ's redeeming love. Then, in times of future hardship, your children will recognize and recall that blessings aren't something they can buy, but are found in their relationships and in the faith that sustains them in any situation.

> **I thought that once we were out of the baby stage, parenting would be a breeze.**
>
> —TORI SPELLING

8. The moment: The parents of one of your daughter's high school senior friends have rented a vacation home on the beach for spring break and are allowing their daughter to invite a group of girls to be their guests. The parents won't be staying at the home, but will be at a different house nearby. You are vehemently opposed to the spring break "rite of passage," but if you don't permit her to go, your daughter will be the only one in her group of friends who misses out. You feel parents who have more money than sense are cornering you into a decision you don't want to make. What lessons will your decision teach? And what do you tell your senior?

Why on earth would a parent object to the idea of letting loose a houseful of lovely, innocent teenage girls on a beach for spring break? What could possibly go wrong?

Giving teens the opportunity to spread their wings and fly doesn't mean you should knowingly send them into harm's way. The goal is to teach them how to evaluate risk and make smart decisions to protect their safety, while giving them experiences that make life richer and more fun. So this is one of those situations where the right answer is: It all depends.

I wouldn't have let my teens go on a spring break trip to Cancun (no one ever asked, because, *seriously?*), but I was willing to let my son and his two best buddies drive from Michigan to Vermont for a summer running camp. I was the only parent who was willing, so they didn't go, but still. It's not that all travel or adventure is bad, it's that certain situations are more likely to be compromising or create opportunities to make bad decisions. Saying no to those is called "avoiding the near occasion of sin"—always a good strategy.

There are certainly high schoolers who are capable of enjoying a wholesome beach vacation with minimal adult supervision; who won't use this freedom to drink to excess, hook up with people they just met, or get generally crazy; and who will even remember to use sunscreen and call home to check in at least once or twice. I think those three kids should absolutely have the chance to go on spring break together! The rest of all the teenagers in the United States of America should have at least one responsible adult present—in the house, not down the street—to assure that they behave appropriately.

The latest trend in my neck of the woods, however, is for families to congregate in the same resort community for spring break, on the premise that their teens can't go alone and must be supervised. This often results in a dystopian alternative in which everyone misbehaves! It's unlikely you're going to promote positive future behavior if your idea of keeping your kids safe is to travel with them to Panama City and fill the freezer with buckets of premixed margaritas. But such is the culture in which we live. Parents don't want to say no, so they join the party instead. The next thing you know, even moms and dads are posting selfies on Facebook.

Perhaps the most dangerous parental error is adopting the faulty logic that teens are going to make mistakes anyway, so you may as well provide an environment in which the risks are minimized. Think: collecting the car keys and hosting the kegger, or putting a daughter on the pill "just in case." Recalling their own antics, some parents figure a rowdy spring break is a rite of passage that they survived, and their kids may as well experience it, too.

But this isn't the same world in which we parents grew up. We didn't have to worry about predator drugs that allowed for the possibility of "date rape" being slipped into drinks, or Internet sites that make it easy to ruin someone's reputation with a surreptitious video, or a hook-up culture that promotes casual sex and results in epidemic levels of STDs. Add to all of that the alarming level of binge drinking among teens—especially as a time-honored spring break tradition—and the potential for disaster is real.

If partying is a rite of passage, the role of parents is to make it difficult and voice their disapproval. The Partnership for a Drug-Free America has, for years, proven that parental communication about drinking and drug use is a deterrent. Creating opportunities for the very behavior you're trying to discourage is a mixed message that any teen would interpret as permission.

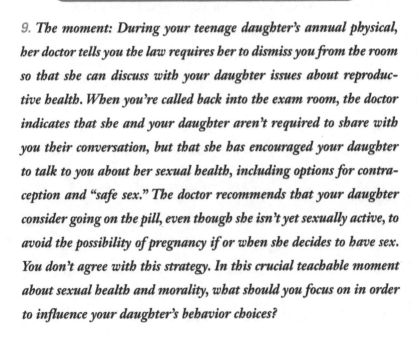

They slipped briskly into an intimacy from which they never recovered.
—F. SCOTT FITZGERALD

9. The moment: During your teenage daughter's annual physical, her doctor tells you the law requires her to dismiss you from the room so that she can discuss with your daughter issues about reproductive health. When you're called back into the exam room, the doctor indicates that she and your daughter aren't required to share with you their conversation, but that she has encouraged your daughter to talk to you about her sexual health, including options for contraception and "safe sex." The doctor recommends that your daughter consider going on the pill, even though she isn't yet sexually active, to avoid the possibility of pregnancy if or when she decides to have sex. You don't agree with this strategy. In this crucial teachable moment about sexual health and morality, what should you focus on in order to influence your daughter's behavior choices?

In a culture where our minor daughters cannot get a tooth filled without parental consent, it remains a conundrum that girls have full access to sexual health care—including hormonal and intrauterine birth control (and in some states, abortion)—without their parents' knowledge or permission. It's a heartbreaking intrusion into the proper relationship between parents and daughters that further deteriorates the stability of families, and sadly, it's a reflection of the cynical belief that teenagers are incapable of practicing self-control over their sexual urges.

Government agencies and health organizations run ad campaigns to encourage teens to say no to drugs, alcohol, cigarettes, and sugary snacks. But apparently, in our culture, we can't imagine that teens might be persuaded to remain chaste. It's the insidious demoralization of low expectations. Don't buy into it.

The progressive view of adolescence would have us believe there are only two kinds of teens: those who use contraception and practice "safe sex" to avoid pregnancy and sexually transmitted diseases, or those who end up pregnant or infected with STDs. There's a third option, and it happens to be the healthiest and most predictive of success in every measurable way: remaining abstinent throughout adolescence, with an eye toward marital sex. This option requires parents to speak openly to their teenagers about their values and expectations.

For our children to be persuaded that our values are better than those espoused by the popular culture, they have to understand our beliefs about sexuality and the proper place for sexual expression. Nowhere are Christian values about this subject more beautifully articulated than in Pope St. John Paul II's seminal writing *Theology of the Body*, a work that resonates not only with Catholic Christians but also with anyone who believes that God's gift of sexuality is part of our essential personhood, intended to uplift our human dignity and lead us to holiness. (See the end notes for a resource to learn more about *Theology of the Body*.)

When they appreciate the sanctity of sexual intimacy, your teens can be empowered by your confidence to practice abstinence. You can remind them, "It might seem difficult to remain abstinent when other kids act like sex is no big deal, but it *is* a big deal, and it can be a negative experience at your age. You don't need to be sexually active as a teenager, and I believe you're capable of self-discipline. Dating is great, and it's meant to be fun and fulfilling at this time in your life, but getting too physical puts a lot of weight on a relationship. And hooking up is just degrading. It would make you feel worse about yourself instead of making you feel sexy and cool."

Don't shy away from candid conversations about sex. Instead, make it a subject about which your teen can talk with you comfortably. Studies prove that parental communication is a powerful tool to promote abstinence. According to the US Department of Health and Human Services Office of Adolescent Health, teens who talk to their parents about sex from an early age are less likely to have sex during their teenage years than kids whose parents avoid such talks. Parental pressure to remain abstinent *does* make a difference.

In the same way, offering to put your teenage daughter on birth control or discussing the importance of condom use with your son also sends a strong message. These actions, which may seem logical and preemptive, actually can signal to your teen that you're delivering the parental "party line" about abstinence, but really, you're saying, "Whatever you do, don't get pregnant." (Or "Don't get a girl pregnant.")

Many parents are led to believe that avoiding teen pregnancy is the single most important goal. Certainly, an unwanted pregnancy during high school or college is a life-changing and defining outcome. No one wants their daughter or son to become a parent at such a young age. But the primary goal ought to be avoiding the onset of an active sex life, not just avoiding pregnancy. For this reason, I believe it's best to keep the focus on abstinence, not on so-called safe sex.

Suppose your son or daughter already is involved in a sexually intimate relationship? Shouldn't you then help them obtain sexual health care and insist they use birth control? At the risk of seeming strident, I don't believe that's the answer. Teens whose romantic relationships become overly intimate need parental guidance to decelerate the relationship. You should step in, but not to make it easier to have sex. Rather, have a frank and adult discussion with your child and his or her boyfriend or girlfriend about the significance of their actions. That conversation should begin, "We know you care very much about each other, but if you love each other as you say you do, you'll stop having sex and putting your futures at risk. Instead, show each other how much you really care about one another by honoring and respecting one another. Take this time to get to know each other's hearts, and let God bless you with maturity and patience while you put your relationship on the right footing. It will require self-discipline, but that's something you will need if you're going to stay together as a couple. If you're meant to be together, it will happen in good time. For now, you can show your love by abstaining from sex."

Oddly enough, our culture treats teens as though they are mini-adults when it comes to sexual behavior, but the idea that parents would sit down with a teenage couple and set out expectations for a mature relationship is viewed as intrusive or "rushing" them into something too serious. What could be more serious than engaging in a sexually intimate love affair? Teens who are "ready" to take that step in a relationship ought to be ready to defend their romance to their parents.

The point is, just because your teenager may have become sexually active doesn't mean you can't influence him or her to decide that abstinence is a better, safer, healthier, and more honorable choice.

If your teen is determined to continue in a sexual relationship, you should insist that he or she exhibit responsibility in this adult decision. You can ask that he or she seek out appropriate advice and counsel from a doctor or clinic, and you should provide information about counseling services in case they are needed. But you shouldn't facilitate access to birth control or other sexual health services if you fundamentally object to your teen's sexual behavior. Instead, say, "I get that you feel this is the best choice for you, but I disagree. I hope you are taking good care of your health, and that you understand the serious ramifications of a sexual relationship. I'm your parent, so I'll always be here for you, but I can't condone your decision, so I'm not able to support you with help in doing something I believe is wrong for you."

Which brings us back to the doctor's office, where we parents often feel like creepy strangers outside an exam room, while a doctor legally usurps our right to oversee our minor children's health care! It's frustrating and insulting to be dismissed while a physician offers your teen information about sex and birth control. Here's what I have said in these circumstances: "It's true that the law requires doctors to have one-on-one talks with teens about sex, but don't ever forget that no one—NO ONE—cares more about your health and well-being than your parents. There is nothing you can't talk to us about, including sex. Especially sex! We know you better than anyone, and we want what is best for you in every situation. Despite the fact that the law allows doctors to dismiss parents from the exam room, you can trust us with your most private concerns and questions. We won't shame you, we won't dismiss your feelings or your fears, and we won't condemn you if you make mistakes. If you felt that you couldn't talk to us, you could certainly get advice from the doctor. In fact, we would encourage that. But we hope you understand that we're here for you no matter what, and especially as you grow and mature into a young adult."

Our hypersexual culture requires parents to be brave and bold. There are many voices telling our teens that because they are sexual beings, they are entitled to enjoy an active sex life for personal gratification and pleasure. But the voices of loving parents can even more powerfully remind children that God's gift of sexuality is meant to be life-giving, affirming, and fulfilling. Open and honest communication is the path to purity for our teens, so keep talking, listening, and loving unconditionally.

I gave in and admitted that God was God.

—C. S. LEWIS

10. The moment: Your daughter is college-bound and excited to be on her own. You are confident she's ready for college, but you are worried that she'll stop going to church while she's away at school. How can you assure that she's involved in her faith, especially at a big public university—an environment that notoriously undermines Christian belief? Is there something you can do to assure she goes to church?

The short answer is: no. Not even attending a Christian college would assure that she's going to church on Sundays, and unless you plan to camp outside your daughter's dorm and forcibly transport her to a pew, you won't be able to assure that she's being spiritually fed each week. Fortunately for you, this isn't even part of God's job description for parents!

You did your part. You raised your young adult daughter in the church and provided a faith-filled home in which she has seen how God reveals himself through love and grace. Now, it's time to let God mold her into a mature Christian. Not that this will be an easy process to watch from the sidelines—and to be clear, I'm not a parent who believes that the job of parenting is "complete" when our kids turn eighteen and "can do whatever they want." (I put that in quotation marks because that's what I do to roll my eyes in print!) We're never done being parents to our children, but our relationships do (and must) change as our children become adults.

When they are little, our role is to require obedience from our children as a way to model the act of obedience to God. For this reason, I think it's cool to require that children who live in your home attend church, even if they're doing so only because it's a requirement of the house.

When they become adults (and leaving for college is certainly a mark of adulthood), our role is to model and demonstrate how we live out the tenets of our faith in our adult lives, and to encourage our children toward greater maturity in their faith. Clearly, it's not mature for a person to go to church while away at school simply because her parents insist that she do so. *She* needs to choose to honor her faith and make it the cornerstone of her adult life. You can't choose that for her.

This is a fearful idea for many parents! They're so focused on the scary "what ifs"—"What if she stops going to church? What if she decides to go to a different church? What if she becomes an agnostic or atheist because of the things she's exposed to in school? What if she rejects us because of the faith we profess?"—that they're not able to imagine this one: "What if the foundation of faith we gave her is enough to withstand the doubts, misgivings, exploration, examination, and thoughtfulness of our young adult daughter?"

Remember that Christianity has withstood the tests of teenagers for more than two thousand years. Jesus isn't afraid of college kids!

When our children leave home to go to college, it's a great teachable moment. So when you take your daughter to school, do these three things:

1. *Talk in the car about how glad you are that she's a faithful person.* Instead of telling her how worried you are about her missing church, ask how she sees herself getting involved in her new faith community. (Note: She should be the one doing the talking!)

2. *Before you take her out for that "last supper" with Mom and Dad, stop in at the campus ministry office.* Virtually every college has one. Meet the staff, collect the in-

formation on Mass or church service times and ministry opportunities, and make sure the brochure (or whatever material they give you) ends up in her dorm room before you leave.

3. *During the semester, don't badger her about whether she's been to church.* She knows you're worried about this, so she'll probably make a point of telling you if she's going. Instead, find ways to gently remind her to pray about the things that are stressing her out, encourage her to stop by the church or chapel to shore up her spirit, and most of all, let her know you're praying for her, each and every day.

Remember, God doesn't bop us over the head and drag us into a relationship with him. He invites! Keep the invitation to faith open for your daughter by reminding her how much God loves her. God will handle the rest.

The Lesson Plan

Offering children the opportunity to grow and mature in the real world takes guts. But brave parenting is the only way to allow children the freedom and responsibility to demonstrate to you—and more importantly, to themselves—that they are capable and self-reliant. If there's a way to measure success in parenting (a nebulous thing to gauge, to be sure), it is a child's independence. Building strong character, a healthy conscience, and a vibrant faith are the keys to maturity and independence.

Here are a few reminders for parenting in the real world:

- *Kids need real-world experiences.* Take a long look at the boundaries you place around your children and consider whether those exist for their safety or your peace of mind. You can't raise self-reliant, independent people inside a bubble, and your over-protected children won't suddenly become self-assured without opportunities to prove to themselves (and to you!) that they are capable. Let loose the reins and see what happens.

- *Let your kids make mistakes.* When we allow children the freedom to be out in the world, they're likely to mess up. Expect this, and don't worry too much. Mistakes are better teachers than any lecture or warning you could ever convey.

- *Character is revealed in hard times.* A good kid doing good things is expected. A good kid who does a dumb thing but steps up and takes responsibility for his or her actions has the potential for greatness. Let your children suffer the consequences for their actions—don't ever mitigate them or justify their bad behavior—and watch the depth of character and conscience that develops.

- *Mature faith is a choice.* Kids face many challenges to their Christian faith—from the academic world, through real-world tragedies, through their own struggles. Encourage your child's deepening faith by modeling it and by always issuing an invitation to encounter Jesus through you. You can't force belief. But you can extend Christ's friendship to your children in a way that makes them want it for themselves. If you do that, one day you're going to hear a resounding, "Well done!"

CHAPTER EIGHT

The Moments That Matter

F THE TASK OF imparting values and virtue seems daunting, take heart. God knows we're not perfect parents. He also knows there is only one perfect child: his Son. And though parents are called to do the work of instilling character and conscience, and to pass our faith along to our children, it's not up to us to determine our success. That's up to God, since he's the only one who can see into our children's hearts and souls.

God knows that our service to him as parents is made all the more challenging by the culture in which we live. Our modern age allows us to enjoy the benefits of education, technology, health and longevity, mobility, and prosperity. Yet we struggle to attend to the most basic and necessary aspects of child-rearing. The distractions are too great, and our priorities too easily confused. But the impact of our cultural immersion on children and families is measurable and meaningful, and gradually, it is revealing a nation wanting for skilled and solid parenting.

I've spent the better part of ten years writing and speaking about the effect of parenting in America. In my effort to communicate the urgency of our cultural dilemma, much of what I have said is challenging. I've blamed parents for allowing their kids to become rude and materialistic, oversexualized and undereducated. I've pointed the finger at parents for myriad issues, from childhood obesity and the entitlement mentality to the proliferation of porn addiction in young men and the hook-up culture on college campuses. I even theorized, in my only viral column, that the Occupy Wall Street movement was a cultural indicator of bad parenting. And I've maintained for years that the grand governmental experiment we call America is at risk of failing unless parents raise up a new generation of patriots like those who founded our great nation.

Imagine my chagrin, then, when during one radio interview, I was challenged with a question about nature over nurture. "Isn't it true that parents really don't have that much control over how their kids turn out," the questioner said, "because kids' personalities and character are already established by their DNA? In fact, studies of identical twins separated at birth prove that they turn out about the same, even though they're raised by different parents. So your claim that parenting makes all the difference seems overstated. Why put so much pressure on parents?"

I didn't have a ready answer, so I did that thing politicians do: I stalled. "Good question," I said, "I'm really glad you asked."

It *is* a good question. The roles of nature and nurture in human development have been studied and considered since the beginnings of science. The nativist theory asserts that we are the way we are because of our genes, and our DNA is the code that explains our character and personalities. The environmentalist theory says we are the way we are because of the way we are raised, coupled with our life experiences. It supposes us all to be blank slates, on which our parents and the environments in which we live etch the attributes that define our character.

In reality, it's both. God creates every person with a unique and miraculous design—one that is revealed in personality and temperament. But then he entrusts parents to mold and develop the traits that define a child, informing his actions, choices, and pursuits.

It seems silly to ask, "Does parenting make a difference?" Of course it does! Despite the claims of geneticists, and even without looking to the proof offered by behavioral scientists, we know that the relationship between mothers, fathers, and their children can be either an enormous advantage or a serious hindrance in a child's young life and beyond. Not to mention, parenting is learned and repeated. How we go about the work of raising children is enormously important to our kids as individuals, but also to the society they will one day inherit and lead.

This is why it's so important that we keep our focus on our children's interior character and the formation of conscience, rather than on assuring that they achieve success in all of their childhood endeavors. We can't anticipate what the future holds, so we must empower our children with the values and virtues they will need no matter what lies ahead. "Preparing the child for the path" means equipping them emotionally, intellectually, physically, and especially spiritually to meet the challenges that God allows in the years to come.

Yes, our parenting matters. Moreover, we are obliged to approach the roles of motherhood or fatherhood with a sense of duty to the One who chose us for this essential work. We won't answer to our children or even to society for our efforts as parents; we will answer to God.

The Reason for Parenthood

What does it mean to fulfill our parental obligations? What constitutes strong, effective parenting?

If you read parenting websites and magazines, you'll find lots of information about the "job" of parenting. It's our job to be caretakers for our children, to keep them safe, and to meet their needs. It's our responsibility to love them and lead them to adulthood. It's our job to see that they're educated, well-behaved, and well-mannered. According to the experts, doing a "good job" means our children are well-adjusted, successful, and most of all, happy.

Behavior modification is also a parent's "job." Modern-day parenting advice focuses on getting kids to cooperate, reducing their experiences of frustration, anticipating their reactions, offering choices rather than giving directions, and using systems of positive reinforcement and rewards to reinforce the behaviors that parents want. It sounds a lot like training a dog. In fact, it is. That's why this sort of parenting works well with wee ones. A well-parented toddler should behave similarly to a well-trained golden retriever.

But there's much more to parenting than managing a child's behaviors. Or at least, there should be. The real "job" of parenting is the molding of a child's character and the formation of the heart. A kid with great character behaves like a great kid, so in that sense, working on a child's interior development is also the best way to get that child to act as you'd like.

My journalistic cynicism aside, you have to wonder what motivates some parents. As we have seen, too many are consumed with their children's happiness and don't seem to give a thought about their character, as if a child's happiness on any given day were the measure of parental love and provision. These parents take on the role of servant to their children, fulfilling their kids' wants and desires, rather than leading them toward maturity and independence. For others, having children, in addition to being a path to family and fulfillment, also represents some level of personal achievement. These parents are driven by their children's accomplishments, and they engage in parenting as a competitive endeavor in which every aspect of life is open to comparison and improvement. Their kid's successes in sports, music, and the arts, as well as in school and on standardized tests, are all seen as reflections of their parental acumen.

The notion that children are twenty-first-century "trophies" impacts the character of our youngest generation. The growing sense of entitlement that children exhibit, coupled with an ill-formed conscience, promotes behavior that can be unappealing at best, and unconscionable at worst.

Wanting good things for our children doesn't necessarily mean we have impure motives. We all want our kids to succeed academically and in other areas, and to be well-regarded by their friends, teachers, and the community. But this focus on happiness and on getting kids to "do their best" often means we're not teaching them how to *be* their best. Yet that's what God intends for parents to do.

God's Plan for Parents

For Christians, parenting is not a "job." Rather, it's a response to God's call to parenthood. God leads you to your spouse, and then puts the desire for children in your hearts so that your marriage can be used for his creative purposes. By definition, Christian parenthood is a "vocation"—something you feel drawn to do that lets you use your life to serve God.

In our society, the notion that parenthood is a vocation seems almost quaint. But in reality, viewing parenthood as a vocation is a profound way to understand our responsibilities with respect to our children.

God, being God, could have created us any way he desired. He didn't have to design us as creatures of dependency, but he did. He specifically intended us to be born of both a mother and a father, and to need them (or someone in their stead) in order to survive. God gives us this fundamental relationship because it most closely approximates his love for us and mimics, exactly, the relationship he modeled for us with his Son, Jesus Christ.

The unconditional love of parents for their children is perhaps the purest, most instinctive love we experience. Yet, similar to the way God interacts with us, we parents also instruct and discipline our children precisely *because* we love them. Hebrews 12:6 reminds us, "For whom the Lord loves he disciplines." (We parents say things like, "This is going to hurt me more than it's going to hurt you.")

We're meant to provide our children with experiences in obedience so that by learning to obey us, they'll learn to obey God.

In addition to loving, protecting, and disciplining our children, God means for us to teach them not to need us. If we're successful as parents, we'll raise children who are independent, self-sufficient, and self-directed.

Perhaps most importantly, God created a system in which we parents must teach our children the moral and ethical codes they will need to navigate the world. They may have innate personalities and characteristics, but children are not born knowing what's good or bad, right or wrong. The family system that God designed is meant to put parents in an authoritative role, lovingly leading and molding our children to know, love, and serve God, and to live moral lives that reflect good, godly character.

Teachable Moments for Parents, Too

The vocation of parenthood is meant to accomplish the job of formation of children, but God doesn't leave it at that. Even as we mold and teach our kids about character, conscience, and faith, we're also being transformed by our experiences as parents.

In a perfect symbiotic relationship, we lead our children to God, and they lead us in return.

Bless their little hearts, but the path they forge for us often is paved with fear.

Every parent knows the feeling of helplessness and anxiety that accompanies the love of a child. I can close my eyes and watch a slide show of my darkest, most terrifying moments: Kate being loaded into an ambulance after a post-tonsillectomy bleed that nearly took her life; Betsy going missing for several hours in the neighborhood while we searched from house to house to find her; Jimmy flipping and kicking on an ultrasound screen in the midst of a dangerously precarious pregnancy; Amy, burning with fever and clinging to me as I walked her and an IV pole through the halls of the pediatric unit. In each of those instances and countless others, I could only pray, "Please, God, please . . ."

I didn't have to tell him what I wanted. He knows better than any of us the grueling pain of watching a child suffer.

In perhaps the most ironic twist of all, God grants us the immense honor and joy of parenting our children, but he demands that we accept that they don't really belong to us; they belong to him. And so from the day you learn you are going to have a child, be it through your own pregnancy or adoption, you pray for his or her safety and for the strength to serve God, and not your own heart. But there's a bonus: a windfall of grace and mercy that comes with the territory. By suffering with and for our children, we're brought closer to the God who chooses us to participate in the miracle of creation.

Our children teach us to love like God loves, to see Jesus in others, to invite the Holy Spirit into our hearts. They cause us to bear suffering for love's sake, to exhibit patience, and kindness, and compassion. They offer us opportunities for humility and meekness, magnanimity and wisdom. Their dependency compels our strength; their innocence demands our protection. They require everything and nothing.

They are the living, breathing evidence of how deeply God loves us.

The Moments That Matter

I remember the moment when I became overwhelmed by mother-hood for the first time. Kate, my eldest, was four days old, sleeping sweetly in a handmade cradle in our family room. I sat on the couch, watching the gentle cadence of her breathing, contemplating the tiny wrinkles on her brow, and wallowing in a flood of hormones and sleep deprivation. I was unable to do anything but stare at the little creature who now controlled my every coherent thought . . . and cry.

That's when it hit me: the realization that my capacity to love this unique human being was then only matched by the possibility of heartache that occupied my deepest fears. She was no longer the the-oretical "new baby," she was "Baby Katie," and she had changed me forever. She had redefined me. She had turned me into a mother, and I would never be the same.

Through whimpers and soggy Kleenex, I recall saying to my fa-ther, who sat across the room reading a book, "I know this is going to sound ridiculous, but I'm just now realizing that parenting an-other person is a huge responsibility. There are so many ways I could screw up."

My dad, a father of six who is not given to psychological analysis, just said: "Well, you can't love kids too much. Just love her and she'll be fine."

I can't recount how many times in the past twenty-four years I have taken comfort in that simple yet profound wisdom. At times when I've been uncertain about what to do or say to guide and teach my children—or more often, when I'm sure I did or said exactly the wrong thing—I remember that moment. I was a vulnerable new mom, overcome by the weight of the role I was called to play in the life of my daughter, and my father gave me the confidence to rely on my capacity for love.

My dad doesn't have any recollection of that brief encounter, in which, even as an adult, my character was shaped by his insight. It was just a moment; just a brief conversation that arose in the natural unfolding of a day. He never set out to instruct me about how to overcome my fears, and I surely didn't mean to seek his advice while bawling on the couch in between feedings. But I never forgot it.

That's the essence of a teachable moment.

In the end, you'll never know which moments mattered most in your child's life. Through the years, I've delivered what I thought were monologues of maternal greatness that I know my kids tuned out, while my comments made in passing were often the very coaching or encouragement they needed to imprint their hearts with a lesson borne of love.

So it turns out Dad was right. In every moment, as you help your children become the people God created them to be, all you're really called to do is love them.

God will do the rest.

Acknowledgments

NEVER PLANNED TO WRITE a fourth book, but God had other plans.

Early in 2013, I found myself at a professional crossroads, trying to discern in what direction my career should go. One evening, I called my mom and asked her to pray for me. I knew that if my mother interceded for me, the Lord would grant whatever grace she requested, for no one understands the love of a mother like our Savior, Jesus Christ.

Shortly after she began praying for me, the offer to write this book surfaced *out of nowhere*. It was clear to me that I was being called to refocus my writing on the subject of parenting and share with readers the experiences and insights I've gained in my vocation of motherhood and my profession as a culture commentator.

So I will begin my acknowledgments by saying thank you, Polly Brennan, for praying for me. Thank you for being the most inspiring example of womanhood that I could hope to emulate. Thanks for your pep talks, and your confidence, and your certainty that everything works out. More than anything, thank you for teaching me how to fulfill my vocation so that I can serve our God by serving my family.

My dad, Tom Brennan, is a loving and committed father. Dad, thanks for supporting my family and me in every way imaginable, and especially for the model you and Mom have offered all of us of lifelong marriage and devoted parenthood.

Sometimes, an answered prayer is a good literary agent. The patient and professional Craig Wiley of The Wiley Agency, to whom I am grateful for wise counsel and enthusiastic support, led me to Howard Books.

I'm grateful to all the folks there, but especially Vice President and Editor in Chief Becky Nesbitt for choosing this book and enabling me to share my parenting perspective. I'm honored to join Howard's roster of authors that includes the Robertson family. I now have serious street cred with my husband, an avid *Duck Dynasty* fan.

Becky didn't only agree to publish this book, she gave me the gift of an exceptional editor in Liz Heaney. Liz is like a literary midwife. She coaxes the thing out of you, all the while telling you what a great job you are doing, even when you're crying and making excuses and missing all of your deadlines. Excellence in editing is making an author better than she is. Liz is excellent.

I am also grateful to Rose Judson, whose expert copyediting and thoughtful suggestions improved my manuscript.

I'm blessed with a big, supportive family and a host of dear friends, all of whom encouraged me over the long months of writing. Special thanks to the Brennans, Radelets, Campbells, Footes, Liesmans, Heberliens, and Krupps.

Thank you, Kate Hicks, for your stalwart faith in me; Betsy Hicks, for wisdom beyond your years; Jimmy Hicks, for unbridled affection; and Amy Hicks, for believing that I'm the strongest person you know. I am grateful to you, and for you. I hope you can see in the pages of this book how much I love you. One thing is certain: You four prove to me that God loves me beyond measure.

Finally, thank you, Jim Hicks, for your trust, support, and devotion. You are an exemplary husband, an extraordinary father, and my dearest friend in all the world. I know I'm meant to help you get to heaven, but you are helping me more. I love you.

Marybeth Hicks
January 16, 2014
East Lansing, Michigan

Bibliography

CHAPTER ONE

"Boy, 12, Sentenced In Shopping Cart Drop At Harlem Target." CBS New York. March 8, 2012. Accessed November 25, 2013. http://newyork.cbslocal.com/2012/03/08/12-year-old-sentenced-in-harlem-shopping-cart-drop/.

Brooks, David. "If It Feels Good . . ." *The New York Times*, September 13, 2011. Accessed November 25, 2013. http://www.nytimes.com/2011/09/13/opinion/if-it-feels-right.html?_r=0.

"Bullying Allegations Probed after Boy, 15, Commits Suicide after First Day of School." Fox News. August 29, 2013. Accessed November 25, 2013. http://www.foxnews.com/us/2013/08/29/bullying-allegations-probed-after-boy-15-commits-suicide-after-first-day-school/.

Halbfinger, David M., and Beth Kormanik. "Rutgers Case Jurors Call Digital Evidence Crucial." *The New York Times*, March 16, 2012. Accessed November 25, 2013. http://www.nytimes.com/2012/03/17/nyregion/jurors-say-digital-evidence-convinced-them-of-dharun-ravis-guilt.html?_r=0.

Josephson Institute of Ethics, Character Counts! Coalition. "For the First

Time in a Decade, Lying, Cheating and Stealing Among American Students Drops." News release, November 20, 2012. Character Counts.org. Accessed November 25, 2013. http://charactercounts .org/pdf/reportcard/2012/ReportCard-2012-PressRelease-Honesty IntegrityCheating.pdf.

Pond, Allison, Gregory Smith, and Scott Clement. "Religion Among the Millennials." Pew Research Center's Religion & Public Life Project. February 17, 2010. Accessed November 25, 2013. http://www.pew forum.org/2010/02/17/religion-among-the-millennials/.

Prager, Dennis. "Why Young Americans Can't Think Morally." National Review Online. September 20, 2011. Accessed November 25, 2013. http://www.nationalreview.com/articles/277693/why-young-ameri cans-can-t-think-morally-dennis-prager.

Rideout, Victoria J., Ulla G. Foehr, and Donald F. Roberts. *Generation M2: Media in the Lives of 8- to 18-Year-Olds.* Report. January 20, 2010. Accessed November 25, 2013. http://kaiserfamilyfoundation.files.word press.com/2013/04/8010.pdf.

Robb Jackson, Mary. "Grove City 11-Year-Old Found 'Sexting' Topless Photos." CBS Pittsburgh. July 9, 2013. Accessed November 25, 2013. http://pittsburgh.cbslocal.com/2013/07/09/grove-city-11-year-old-found-sexting-topless-photos/.

CHAPTER TWO

Sajna, Mike. "Talking Back." *University Times* (University of Pittsburgh), November 6, 1997. Accessed November 25, 2013. http://www.utimes .pitt.edu/?p=3279.

CHAPTER THREE

Donvan, John, and Mary-Rose Abraham. "Is the Internet Driving Pornography Addiction Among School-Aged Kids?" ABC News—*Nightline.* May 8, 2012. Accessed November 25, 2013. http://abcnews.go.com/ Technology/internet-driving-pornography-addiction-school-aged-kids/story?id=16297026&singlePage=true.

"Five Key Questions and Core Concepts of Media Literacy for Deconstruction." Center for Media Literacy, 2011. Accessed November 25, 2013. http://www.medialit.org/sites/default/files/14A_CCKQposter .pdf

"Impact of Music, Music Lyrics, and Music Videos on Children and

Youth." *Pediatrics* 124, no. 5 (November 1, 2009): 1488-494. Accessed November 25, 2013. doi:10.1542/peds.2009-2145.

Le, Bryan. "Is Video Gaming the End-Boss of Digital Addictions?" The Fix. April 22, 2013. Accessed November 25, 2013. http://www.the fix.com/content/video-gaming-Internet-addiction-digital-revolu tion-DSM-5505.

Parents Television Council. "Happily Never After: New PTC Study Reveals TV Favors Non-Marital Sex." News release, August 5, 2008. Parents Television Council. Accessed November 25, 2013. https://www.parentstv.org/PTC/news/release/2008/0805.asp.

Pond, Allison, Gregory Smith, and Scott Clement. "Religion Among the Millennials." Pew Research Center's Religion & Public Life Project. February 17, 2010. Accessed November 25, 2013. http://www.pew forum.org/2010/02/17/religion-among-the-millennials/.

Rankin, Russ. "Fewer Americans Believe Homosexuality Is a Sin." LifeWay Christian Resources. January 10, 2013. Accessed November 25, 2013. http://www.lifeway.com/Article/News-fewer-americans-believe-homosexuality-is-a-sin.

Salmond, Kimberlee, and Judy Schoenberg. *Good Intentions: The Beliefs and Values of Teens and Tweens Today*. Report. New York: Girl Scouts of the USA, Girl Scout Research Institute, 2009. Accessed November 25, 2013. http://www.girlscouts.org/research/pdf/good_intentions_full_report.pdf.

Simmons College. "Violent Video Games Can Hinder Development, Simmons Study Finds." News release, April 4, 2011. Accessed November 25, 2013. http://www.simmons.edu/overview/about/news/press/1013.php.

Smietana, Bob. "Survey: Big Drop in Those Who Say Being Gay's a Sin." *USA Today*, January 11, 2013. Accessed November 25, 2013. http://www.usatoday.com/story/news/2013/01/10/poll-minority-says-being-gays-a-sin/1825461/.

CHAPTER FOUR

"Bullying Prevention Resources." Josephson Institute Center for Youth Ethics. Accessed November 25, 2013. http://charactercounts.org/resources/youthviolence/.

"Fact Sheets—Underage Drinking." Centers for Disease Control and Prevention. December 26, 2012. Accessed November 25, 2013. http://www.cdc.gov/alcohol/fact-sheets/underage-drinking.htm.

Gurian, Anita, and Alice Pope. "Do Kids Need Friends?" AboutOurKids. org. Accessed November 25, 2013. http://www.aboutourkids.org/ articles/do_kids_need_friends.

Hicks, Marybeth. *Don't Let the Kids Drink the Kool-Aid: Confronting the Assault on Our Families, Faith, and Freedom.* Washington, DC: Regnery, 2011.

Lickona, Thomas. "Prevent Bullying, Promote Kindness: 20 Things All Schools Can Do." *Excellence & Ethics*, September 26, 2012, 1–4. Accessed November 25, 2013. http://www.catholiceducation.org/articles/ education/ed0486.htm.

Madden, Mary, Amanda Lenhart, Maeve Duggan, Sandra Cortesi, and Urs Gasser. "Teens and technology 2013." Pew Research Center Internet Project. March 13, 2013. Accessed November 25, 2013. http://www.pew internet.org/Reports/2013/Teens-and-Tech.aspx.

Miniño, Arialdi M. "Mortality Among Teenagers Aged 12–19 Years: United States, 1999–2006." Centers for Disease Control and Prevention. May 5, 2010. Accessed November 25, 2013. http://www.cdc.gov/ nchs/data/databriefs/db37.htm.

Nelson, Brent V., Troy H. Patience, and David C. MacDonald. "Adolescent Risk Behavior and the Influence of Parents and Education." *Journal of the American Board of Family Medicine* 12, no. 6 (November 1, 1999): 436–43. Accessed November 25, 2013. doi:10.3122/ jabfm.12.6.436.

"Parents Have More Influence over Their Child than Friends, Music, TV, the Internet, and Celebrities." The Partnership at Drugfree.org. Accessed November 25, 2014. http://www.drugfree.org/prevent.

Reisser, Paul C. "Bullying." In *The Focus on the Family Complete Guide to Baby and Child Care.* Tyndale House Publishers, 1999. Accessed November 25, 2013. http://www.focusonthefamily.com/parenting/ schooling/bullying.aspx.

Schmidt, William. "New Anti-Bullying Resources Available for Grades 4–8." Alliance for Catholic Education, University of Notre Dame. September 26, 2011. Accessed November 25, 2013. http://ace.nd.edu/ news/new-anti-bullying-resources-available-for-grades-4-8.

"Sex, Drugs, And Alcohol: Parents Still Influence College Kids' Risky Behavior, Study Shows." *ScienceDaily.* February 11, 2008. Accessed November 25, 2013. http://www.sciencedaily.com/releases/ 2008/02/080210094643.htm.

"Sexual Risk Behavior: HIV, STD, & Teen Pregnancy Prevention." Centers for Disease Control and Prevention. August 26, 2013. Accessed November 25, 2013. http://www.cdc.gov/HealthyYouth/sexual behaviors/.

"Teen Suicide, Facts for Families No. 10." American Academy of Child and Adolescent Psychiatry. May 2008. Accessed November 25, 2013. http://www.aacap.org/AACAP/Families_and_Youth/Facts_for_Families/Facts_for_Families_Pages/Teen_Suicide_10.aspx.

Wiseman, Rosalind. *Queen Bees and Wannabes: Helping Your Daughter Survive Cliques, Gossip, Boyfriends, and the New Realities of Girl World.* New York: Harmony, 2009.

CHAPTER FIVE

Associated Press. "Atheist Family Wants Pledge of Allegiance Banned in Mass. Public Schools." *New York Post*, September 4, 2013. Accessed November 25, 2013. http://nypost.com/2013/09/04/athiest-family-wants-pledge-of-allegiance-banned-in-mass-public-schools/.

Barrett, Natasha. "D.C. Sex Education Test the First of Its Kind in America." WJLA. September 15, 2011. Accessed November 25, 2013. http://www.wjla.com/articles/2011/09/d-c-sex-education-test-the-first-of-its-kind-in-america-66570.html.

Edelman, Susan. "School Pulls Patriotic Song at Graduation, but Justin Bieber's 'Baby' Is OK." *New York Post*. June 10, 2012. Accessed November 26, 2013. http://nypost.com/2012/06/10/school-pulls-patriotic-song-at-graduation-but-justin-biebers-baby-is-ok/.

"First Amendment: Freedom of Religion." United States Courts. Accessed November 25, 2013. http://www.uscourts.gov/educational-resources/get-involved/constitution-activities/first-amendment/freedom-religion.aspx.

Forand, Rebecca. "Risqué Summer Reading Selections Have Parents Upset, School Officials Scrapping Books in Monroe Township." NJ.com. April 22, 2011. Accessed November 25, 2013. http://www.nj.com/gloucester-county/index.ssf/2011/08/monroe_twp_parents_angry_over.html.

Hager, Christina. "N.H. Parents Object To 'Offensive' Book." CBS Boston. December 7, 2010. Accessed November 26, 2013. http://boston.cbslocal.com/2010/12/07/nh-parents-ask-for-book-to-be-removed-from-class/.

"'Helicopter Parents' Stir up Anxiety, Depression." Indiana University Newsroom. 2007. Accessed November 26, 2013. http://newsinfo.iu.edu/web/page/normal/6073.html.

Hicks, Marybeth. *Don't Let the Kids Drink the Kool-Aid: Confronting the Assault on Our Families, Faith, and Freedom*. Washington, DC: Regnery, 2011.

"Hundreds Prepare Protest against Islam Chapter in Volusia Co. School Textbook." WFTV Central Florida. November 4, 2013. Accessed November 26, 2013. http://www.wftv.com/news/news/local/hundreds-prepare-protest-against-islam-chapter-vol/nbhJt/.

Josephson Institute of Ethics, Character Counts! Coalition. "For the First Time in a Decade, Lying, Cheating and Stealing Among American Students Drops." News release, November 20, 2012. Character Counts.org. Accessed November 25, 2013. http://charactercounts.org/pdf/reportcard/2012/ReportCard-2012-PressRelease-Honesty IntegrityCheating.pdf.

Lawrence, Julia. "Number of Homeschoolers Growing Nationwide." Education News. May 21, 2012. Accessed November 25, 2013. http://www.educationnews.org/parenting/number-of-homeschoolers-growing-nationwide/.

"'Legally Blonde' High School Production Causes Controversy." WLWT Cincinnati. December 15, 2012. Accessed November 26, 2013. http://www.wlwt.com/news/local-news/hamilton-county/-Legally-Blonde-high-school-production-causes-controversy/-/13550662/17773264/-/rg4i0iz/-/index.html.

Levesque, Brody. "Fort Worth Student Serves Suspension for Saying 'Homosexuality Is Wrong.'" LGBTQ Nation. September 23, 2011. Accessed November 25, 2013. http://www.lgbtqnation.com/2011/09/fort-worth-student-serves-suspension-for-saying-homosexuality-is-wrong/.

McCormack, Simon. "Dan Savage Speech Controversy: 'It Gets Better' Creator Offends Christian Students." *The Huffington Post*. April 28, 2012. Accessed November 26, 2013. http://www.huffingtonpost.com/2012/04/28/dan-savage-speech-controversy_n_1461863.html.

McCoy, Adam W. "SHS Drama to Stage Controversial Production of 'Spring Awakening.'" Shorewood Patch. March 8, 2013. Accessed November 26, 2013. http://shorewood.patch.com/groups/schools/p/shs-drama-to-stage-controversial-production-of-spring-awakening.

McGuinness, William. "'The Most Fabulous Story Ever Told' At Pioneer Valley Performing Arts School Draws Complaints." *The Huffington Post*. March 7, 2013. Accessed November 26, 2013. http://www.huffingtonpost.com/2013/03/07/the-most-fabulous-story-ever-told-protest_n_2829599.html.

Northwest Ordinance, July 13, 1787 (National Archives Microfilm Publication M332, roll 9); Miscellaneous Papers of the Continental Congress, 1774–89; Records of the Continental and Confederation Congresses and the Constitutional Convention, 1774–89, Record Group 360; National Archives. http://www.ourdocuments.gov/doc.php?flash=true&doc=8

Pacific Justice Institute. "Alameda Parents File Suit Over Denial of Opt-out Requests." News release, August 12, 2009. Pacific Justice Institute. Accessed November 26, 2013. http://www.pacificjustice.org/1/post/2009/08/alameda-parents-file-suit-over-denial-of-opt-out-requests.html.

"Position Statements—Human Sexuality." SIECUS: Sexuality Information and Education Council of the United States. Accessed November 25, 2013. http://www.siecus.org/index.cfm?fuseaction=Page.viewPage&pageId=494&parentID=472.

Potts, Chris. "Brian's Song." *Truth & Triumph* Vol. IV, Issue 3. (November 9, 2011). Accessed November 26, 2013. http://www.alliancedefendingfreedom.org/Faith-and-Justice/4-3/coverstory.

Rawlings, Nate. "Court To Hear From Students Suspended For Wearing American Flag Shirts On Cinco de Mayo." *Time*. October 17, 2013. Accessed November 26, 2013. http://nation.time.com/2013/10/17/court-to-hear-from-students-suspended-for-wearing-american-flag-shirts-on-cinco-de-mayo/.

Roffman, Deborah. *Talk to Me First: Everything You Need to Know to Become Your Kids' "Go-To" Person About Sex.* Boston: Da Capo Lifelong Books, July 2012.

"SexEd Library—Lesson Plans for Every Topic and Everyone." SexEd Library, a Project of SIECUS. Accessed November 26, 2013. http://www.sexedlibrary.org/index.cfm?pageId=722.

"State Policies on Sex Education in Schools." National Conference of State Legislatures. July 1, 2013. Accessed November 25, 2013. http://www.ncsl.org/research/health/state-policies-on-sex-education-in-schools.aspx.

"Students Don't Have to Leave Their Faith at Home." Alliance Defending Freedom. Accessed November 26, 2013. http://www.alliancedefendingfreedom.org/issues/public-education.

Unruh, Bob. "Crossdressing Cafeteria Worker Turns Stomachs of Parents, Kids." WorldNet Daily. September 23, 2011. Accessed November 25, 2013. http://www.wnd.com/2011/09/348033/.

CHAPTER SIX

Bingham, Trista, and Juli Carlos-Henderson. *Los Angeles County Transgender Population Estimates 2012.* Report. February 13, 2013. Accessed November 26, 2013. http://publichealth.lacounty.gov/wwwfiles/ph/hae/hiv/Transgender Population Estimates 2-12-13 pub.pdf.

Crotty, James Marshall. "Fit Kids Score 30% Higher on Tests, But Are Turning Against Sports. Do Adults Need a Timeout?" *Forbes.* September 20, 2012. http://www.forbes.com/sites/jamesmarshallcrotty/2012/09/20/athletically-fit-kids-score-30-higher-on-standardized-tests-but-many-are-turning-against-sports-heres-what-we-can-do/.

Gorman, Fitzalan. "A High School Athlete's GPA vs. Average High School Student's GPA." Everyday Life. June 2013. Accessed November 26, 2013. http://everydaylife.globalpost.com/high-school-athletes-gpa-vs-average-high-school-students-gpa-3702.html.

Hedstrom, Ryan, and Daniel Gould. *Research in Youth Sports: Critical Issues Status* White Paper Summaries of the Existing Literature.* Report. November 1, 2004. Accessed November 26, 2013. http://www.educ.msu.edu/ysi/project/CriticalIssuesYouthSports.pdf.

Hendershott, Anne. "The Transgender Culture Wars." *The Catholic World Report.* August 27, 2013. Accessed November 26, 2013. http://www.catholicworldreport.com/Item/2527/the_transgender_culture_wars.aspx#.UokqJKUwJg0.

Jayson, Sharon. "Each Family Dinner Adds up to Benefits for Adolescents." *USA Today.* March 24, 2013. Accessed November 26, 2013. http://www.usatoday.com/story/news/nation/2013/03/24/family-dinner-adolescent-benefits/2010731/.

Liberty Mutual Insurance Responsible Sports Program. "Parents and Coaches Express Conflicting Opinions Regarding Priorities In Youth Sports Program." News release, September 17, 2013. Liberty Mutual Insurance Responsible Sports Program. Accessed November 26, 2013. https://responsible-sports.libertymutual.com/article/1733/.

NCAA Research. "Estimated Probability of Competing in Athletics Beyond the High School Interscholastic Level." National Collegiate Athletics Association. September 17, 2012. Accessed November 26, 2013. http://www.ncaa.org/wps/wcm/connect/2ae661004cdcfccf8e12efbcf1b60152/Probability-of-going-pro-methodology_Update2012%5B3%5D.pdf?MOD=AJPERES&CACHEID=2ae661004cdcfccf8e12efbcf1b60152.

"Responsible Sports Parenting Guide: Emotional Tanks." Liberty Mutual

Insurance Responsible Sports Program. Accessed November 26, 2013. https://responsible-sports.libertymutual.com/parenting/responsible-sport-parenting-guide/emotional-tank.

Wyshynski, Greg. "Hockey Dad Attacks 14-year-old Player on Ice; Arrested for Child Abuse, Say Police." Yahoo Sports. October 25, 2013. Accessed November 26, 2013. http://sports.yahoo.com/blogs/nhl-puck-daddy/hockey-dad-attacks-14-old-player-ice-arrested-163609491—nhl.html.

"Youth Sports Statistics." Statistic Brain. September 10, 2013. Accessed November 26, 2013. http://www.statisticbrain.com/youth-sports-statistics/.

CHAPTER SEVEN

American Institute of CPAs. "AICPA Survey Reveals What Parents Pay Kids for Allowance, Grades." News release, August 22, 2012. AICPA. Accessed November 26, 2013. http://www.aicpa.org/Press/Press Releases/2012/Pages/AICPA-Survey-Reveals-What-Parents-Pay-Kids-for-Allowance-Grades.aspx.

Black, Rosemary. "Your Kid's a Liar? Great! Lying Is Proof of Intelligence in Young Children, Shows Study." *New York Daily News.* May 17, 2010. Accessed November 26, 2013. http://www.nydailynews.com/lifestyle/health/kid-liar-great-lying-proof-intelligence-young-children-shows-study-article-1.122424.

FreeRangeKids.com. Accessed November 26, 2013. http://www.freerangekids.com.

Office of Adolescent Health. "Reproductive Health: Tips for Parents." US Department of Health and Human Services. December 20, 2013. Accessed January 15, 2014. http://www.hhs.gov/ash/oah/adolescent-health-topics/reproductive-health/teen-pregnancy/tips-for-parents.html.

Partnership for a Drug-Free America. "The Partnership at Drugfree.org." Drugfree.org. Accessed November 26, 2013. http://www.drugfree.org/.

Price, Sean. "Straight Talk about the N-Word." *Teaching Tolerance*, Fall 2011. Accessed November 28, 2013. http://www.tolerance.org/magazine/number-40-fall-2011/feature/straight-talk-about-n-word.

Skenazy, Lenore. "Why I Let My 9-Year-Old Ride the Subway Alone." *The New York Sun.* April 1, 2008. Accessed November 26, 2013. http://www.nysun.com/opinion/why-i-let-my-9-year-old-ride-subway-alone/.

Theology of the Body International Alliance. "Theology of the Body."

TheologyOfTheBody.net. 2007. Accessed January 15, 2014. http://www.theologyofthebody.net/.

"The Teen Brain: Still Under Construction." National Institute of Mental Health. 2011. Accessed November 26, 2013. http://www.nimh.nih.gov/health/publications/the-teen-brain-still-under-construction/index.shtml.

US Department of Health and Human Services, Children's Bureau, Child Welfare Information Gateway. *Leaving Your Child Home Alone.* September 2013. Accessed November 26, 2013. https://www.childwelfare.gov/pubs/factsheets/homealone.pdf.

USA TODAY Guide to Kids' Health. "Four Tips for Teaching Your Kids How to Handle Money." *USA Today.* September 1, 2013. Accessed December 4, 2013. http://www.usatoday.com/story/money/personalfinance/2013/09/01/teach-kids-to-handle-money/2749661/.

About the Author

MARYBETH HICKS IS THE founder and editor of OnTheCulture.com, a blog for American women about the things that matter most, and featured columnist in *Catholic Digest* magazine. A frequent commentator on cultural issues, she has appeared on national television outlets including Fox News Channel's *Hannity* and *Fox and Friends*, the *CBS Evening News*, the Christian Broadcasting Network's *700 Club*, and on dozens of national and regional radio programs. Her culture column, Then Again, appeared for nine years in *The Washington Times*. She currently serves on the advisory board of the Parents Television Council, an organization seeking to promote decency on the airwaves. Marybeth and her husband, Jim Hicks, a law professor, make their home in Michigan, and are the parents of four children.